Visual Interface Design for Windows

Visual Interface Design
for Windows

Effective User Interfaces for
Windows 95, Windows NT, and Windows 3.1

Virginia Howlett

WILEY COMPUTER PUBLISHING

John Wiley & Sons, Inc.
New York • Chichester • Brisbane • Toronto • Singapore

Publisher: Katherine Schowalter
Editor: Philip Sutherland
Assistant Editor: Allison Roarty
Managing Editor: Frank Grazioli
Text Design: Ken Sánchez
Composition: North Market Street Graphics, Lancaster, Pa.

This publication is designed to provide accurate and authoritative information in regard to the subject matter covered. It is sold with the understanding that the publisher is not engaged in rendering legal, accounting, or other professional service. If legal advice or other expert assistance is required, the services of a competent professional person should be sought.

Library of Congress Cataloging-in-Publication Data: 3-13-97
Howlett, Virginia.
    Visual interface design for Windows : effective user interfaces
for Windows 95, Windows NT, and Windows 3.1 / Virginia Howlett.
        p.   cm.
    Includes index.
    ISBN 0-471-13419-8 (pbk. : alk. paper)
    1. Graphical user interfaces (Computer systems)   2. Microsoft
Windows (Computer file)   I. Title.
    QA76.9.U83H69   1996
    005.26—dc20   95-48046
                                                       CIP

Printed in the United States of America
10 9 8 7 6 5 4 3 2 1

To Michael, Ana, and Laura

Contents

Preface   ix

Part One   Foundation

  1   An Introduction to Visual Interface Design   3
  2   The Effects of Visual Impact   19
  3   The Process for Designing Visual Interfaces   31
  4   Developing a Visual Interface Design Strategy   39

Part Two   Graphic Design Principles

  5   Universal Design Principles   51
  6   Graphic Information Design Principles   65

Part Three   Visual Perception

  7   An Introduction to the Psychology of Perception   83
  8   Affordances, Realism, and Dimensions   95
  9   Design for the Screen   109

Part Four   Visual Design Elements

  10   Color   123
  11   Icons and Imagery   137
  12   Fonts   149

Part Five Advice, Tips, and Examples

13 Interface Makeovers   163

14 Great Windows Interfaces I Have Met   185

15 Common Pitfalls and How to Avoid Them   199

References   215

Index   221

Preface

This book is a compilation of research I have done and knowledge I have accumulated while leading the visual design of the Windows operating system interface for the last seven years. In that time, I've seen a new profession develop, that of visual interface, or visual interaction, or software product design. For Windows 1.0, a graphic designer was contracted to draw only a few of the icons; beyond that, the system was designed by the engineers who developed it. In contrast, Windows 95 had a whole team of designers, with at least five people focused on the visuals. There has been a sea change in software for personal computers and it has come about quickly. We have moved from a world of technical products designed by engineers to a world of consumer products created by product designers for a mass market audience. That mass market doesn't want to learn the intricacies of the underlying programming of the software they buy. They want to spend less time learning and completing a task, not more. And they're looking for pizzazz; they expect Disney theme park sophistication or the flashy style of MTV. I hope this book will help all the new designers and developers out there who are trying to create great Windows-based products to better serve this demanding audience.

Before I acknowledge the many people who helped me with the book, I'd like to acknowledge something else: my bias. The reader will notice that many of the examples in the book come from Microsoft products. There are two reasons for this: One is that I work at Microsoft, and our products are near at hand and easy for me to obtain. But the second is that Microsoft has done some excellent interface design work, after years of following in the footsteps of others. Nevertheless, I did try to balance the positive with some negative Microsoft examples; I also included several good examples from products developed by other companies. In any case, I hope the reader will forgive my understandable bias.

There are many people I'd like to thank for helping me make this book a reality. First, I owe a big debt to my managers and directors at Microsoft for their kind support: Steve Madigan, Bob Muglia, Mike Maples, and Natalie Yount were all instrumental in making it happen, and Bill Hill allowed me time to see it to completion. I would like to thank my agent, Claudette Moore, for shepherding me through the shoals of the publishing industry. I am also in debt to my editors at John Wiley and Sons, Phil Sutherland, Frank Grazioli, and Allison Roarty, for their insights. But the biggest and most heartfelt thanks go to my most dedicated reviewers: Mark Malamud, Michael Van Kleeck, and Erik Gavriluk, who were always ready to read another draft and who helped immeasurably with their knowledge of user interface design and development. Other reviewers at Microsoft whose comments helped the manuscript were Kevin Schofield and Joseph Matthews; and my technical reviewers, Keith Pleas and Tony Fernandes, gave me a lot of good ideas at the end of the process. Bill Flora generously loaned me his Encarta designs, Erik Gavriluk provided valuable help with artwork. A special thank you goes to my administrative assistants Ana Thornton and Brenda Scott, without whom I would never have finished the art manuscript. The beautiful typography was designed by Ken Sánchez, who patiently created a sophisticated page design.

I'd like to thank Michael for his unwavering support and confidence, and for forgiving my many late nights. And last of all, I'd like to thank my children, Ana and Laura Thornton, for being so understanding, and for just being the best kids, ever.

Part One

Foundation

1

An Introduction to Visual Interface Design

What Is Design?

Design is a broad term that, used in different contexts, can mean very different things. For instance, engineers design the structures of bridges and the code for software programs; they strive, like mathematicians, for an elegant solution. [figure 1.1] Graphic designers, using subtle visual strategies, create typography and images to communicate information

> *Every single thing made by man or woman since the beginning of time has been designed. In other words, some thought, usually combined with basic instinct, has occurred in the decision-making process to decide how the object should work and how it should look.*
>
> **—Sir Terence Conran, in**
> **Industrial Design—**
> **Reflection of a Century**

```
Cairo Development - s sysimage.c
                    d:\nt\private\windows\user\server\sysimage.c
//*
//  Function:   AddEntry
//
//  History:    11-05-93    ErikGav    Created
//
//  Notes:      Optimized LRU aged hash structure; never page faults
//
/**********************************************************************\

IMAGEENTRY* AddEntry(SYSIMAGELIST* piml, CLSID* pClsID, DWORD dwUnique)
{
    IMAGEENTRY *pie, *pie2;
    ULONG ulHash, ulHash2;

    ulHash = Hash(pClsID, dwUnique);

    if (piml->nImages == NUM_IMAGES) {
        // the cache is full—age
        // out the oldest entry

        pie = piml->pOldest;                    // take the place of the oldest
        piml->pOldest = pie->pNewer;            // and reset the oldest ptr
        pie->pNewer->pOlder = NULL;             // new oldest is now the last

        ulHash2 = Hash(&pie->clsid, pie->dwUnique);

        if (piml->ppHashTable[ulHash2]==pie) {
            if (pie->pNextHash == pie) {
                // points to itself;
                // it's the only one in the chain

                piml->ppHashTable[ulHash2] = NULL;
            } else {
                piml->ppHashTable[ulHash2] = pie->pNextHash;
            }
        }

        // splice out the oldest entry from
        // the hash table

        pie2 = pie;

        do
        {
            pie2 = pie2->pNextHash;             // find the predecessor
        }                                       // in the hash list
        while (pie2->pNextHash != pie);
                                    Line 409      Col 1     C              Ins
F1=Help F2=Save F3=New F4=Del F5=Menu F6=Quit F7=Prev F8=Next F9=Load F10=Exit
```

1.1 Sample of code written in Microsoft Visual C++. Screen courtesy of Erik Gavriluk.

3

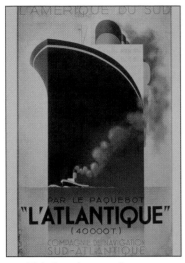

1.2 This French poster by Cassandre from the 1930s is a classic combination of imagery and typography. Photo: Planet Art.

and influence emotion. [figures 1.2 and 1.3] Industrial and product designers focus on the look, shape, and function of household appliances, cars, and furniture, aiming for beauty of form and clarity of purpose. [figure 1.4]

Historically, design is also an element of society and culture. The Incas designed pyramids, the Japanese designed Zen gardens, and Americans designed skyscrapers. The shape of objects and artifacts always reflects the social structure, norms, and aesthetics of their time and place. History, society, culture, and technology all impact the objects themselves. For instance, in his book *Objects of Desire*, Adrian Forty claims the office furniture of the early twentieth century was designed to resemble the factory floor, representing the new, relatively low income and social status of office workers.

Clearly, design is cultural and highly mutable; it is the product of society's ideas, while influencing those ideas. Design encompasses engineering, function, craft, and inevitably has an element of art, style, or aesthetic choice—it ranges from the design of an Indian rug, to the design of the

1.3 This table of contents is from *Interactions,* a quarterly publication of the ACM SIG CHI, which specializes in interface design. Photo courtesy of ACM/Interactions.

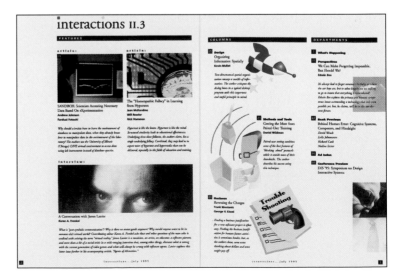

1.4 The Microsoft Natural Keyboard was developed at Microsoft by the Consumer Division's Hardware Industrial Design and Ergonomics Group, along with Ziba Design of Portland, Oregon. It was designed using state of the art research in keyboard design, creating a typing environment that is more comfortable and productive to the end user. Photo: Microsoft.

Brooklyn Bridge, or to the design of Microsoft Excel, and beyond. [figures 1.5, 1.6, and 1.7]

Aspects of Software Interface Design

Software interface design is subtle, and appearance and function are always closely intertwined. It is hard to separate the structural engineering of a product from its behavior or visual presentation. In this book, I will describe design as it applies to the visual makeup of computer

1.5 Note the simple beauty of the native design of a utilitarian object, such as this Indian textile. Photo: Planet Art.

1.6 Although designed for engineering reasons, the Brooklyn Bridge has a soaring beauty. Photo: Leo De Wys, Inc./Henryk T. Kaiser.

1.7 Microsoft Excel for Windows 95, a tool for analyzing numbers, exemplifies a design that is rooted in technology.

software, while acknowledging where the behavioral and engineering aspects of interface design overlap with the visual.

High-quality interface design is particularly important now—and in the future—as personal computers become ubiquitous and the software market develops increasingly sophisticated expectations. The software industry is maturing, both visually and technologically; software has rapidly evolved into a mass-market consumer product from its beginnings as a technical tool used by computer professionals. Consumers demand engaging visuals and very sophisticated ease of use. Only a few years ago, software could be sold completely on technical features, but today customers demand features *and* flash, and the design of the interface can be the deciding factor in a purchase.

In this new era, Windows and Windows-based products will look and feel more like multimedia CD titles, MTV, games, or beautiful books, and less like industrial tools. The static, hard-edged, stamped-metal look is being gradually replaced by soft colors, organic shapes, and complex layers of beautiful text and graphics, which gently animate like leaves in the wind. A single visual style defined by the operating system is being superseded by hundreds of diverse designs, each of which appeals to a unique audience.

Interface Design Strategies

To achieve the ideal combination of engineering and aesthetics, there must be many overlapping design strategies in a software product. These various designs, from the functional specifications to the code to the appearance, build on and influence each other in a complex intertwining of ideas and objectives. The best visual interface design strategy considers and takes advantage of all these elements:

- The tasks the software will support
- The specification and design of the features and functions
- The design of the underlying code structures
- The interaction methods used to access the functions
- The specific visual appearance of the content, functions, and controls
- The overall visual style and communication strategy

Goals of Good Interface Design

There are many important goals for a good Windows interface design. Three that form a good starting point are: design should be intentional, the interface should be unintrusive, and the functional and visual design must have synergy.

Design Should Be Intentional

The quote that begins this chapter points out that human beings often don't realize they are involved with design. In fact, whenever something is made, it is also designed, sometimes with knowledge and forethought, but often without. This subconscious design also is a natural result of the complexities of producing computer programs. A development team that is trying to build a product, and doing the best they can, may inadvertently design poor graphics or poor visual communication. The programmer may have the skills to design elegant, efficient code, but little graphics training to execute the visual manifestations.

Each aspect of the design, from the code to the icons, should be approached with a clear sense of how it impacts the whole, to ensure that it is communicating the intended result. [figure 1.8]

A Good User Interface Is Transparent and Engaging

The best user interface is attractive but not intrusive. Ideally, the user has a pleasant experience—he or she feels invited in, can easily tell what to do, then performs some initial tasks, during which everything works in an intuitive fashion. The interface is barely noticed, except as an attractive, engaging presence.

We have all seen bad user interfaces; they are usually complicated, with lots of bright colors, and they

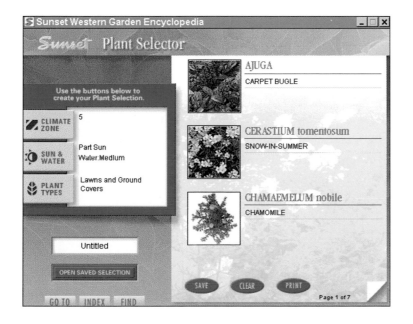

1.8 This screen from the Sunset Western Garden Interactive Guide to Your Yard and Garden has a very intentional design. Every element on the screen contributes to a sophisticated style that evokes a sense of nature, greenery, and quiet.

metaphorically scream "look here!" "look there!" Unfortunately, it's not clear where to start, due to the sheer number of options vying for your attention. When you do finally jump in and try it out, often something unexpected or unwanted occurs and you feel stupid, confused, and not in control. Worse yet is an interface that uses obtuse language you don't understand, which makes you afraid to try something for fear of making a fatal error. We have all used copier machines, VCRs, bank machines, and office telephone systems that were confusing or intimidating. What good is a great feature for double-sided copying if you can't find it or figure out how to use it? [figure 1.9]

Functional Design and Visual Design Must Work Together

Like the buttons on a home appliance, controls in a user interface must look the way they work and work the way they look. [figure 1.10] When the details of the visual design

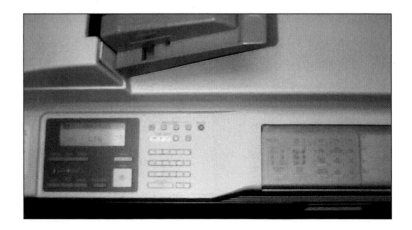

1.9 This copier interface works well in many respects, but because the double-sided copy function is located under a plexiglass cover, some users will never learn how to use it.

clarify the functional intent, the interface becomes "intuitive." An intuitive design builds on the user's experience with the world, makes the most important functions simple and obvious, then progressively discloses more complex functions. In a graphical interface like Microsoft Windows, all functions have a visual component. [figure 1.11] If the visual presentation is at odds with the function, confusion results. For instance, if a button must be clicked for the user to proceed, but the button appears unavailable, the user will get stuck.

When building an interface, it is necessary to consider what the nuances of shape, size, color, and placement of a control communicate to users. How does the design relate to the rest of their experience; how does

1.10 The functions of this familiar home appliance are clearly indicated by its buttons. Black in color, they contrast with the rest of the appliance, and their size and shape invite pushing. Photo: CMCD/Photodisk.

1.11 The three-dimensional buttons and tabs in Windows 95 make the functions of these interface elements more obvious.

it relate to other elements in the program; how does it make the user feel?

Process and Roles in Interface Design

The advent of graphical interfaces and the ever increasing power and sophistication of personal computers have brought big changes to the field of software development. Software design has evolved from being the bailiwick of computer programmers to involving people of many disciplines. We are in the midst of an evolution in the field of computer science, not unlike the one that took place in building construction following the Industrial Revolution. Before the Industrial Revolution, buildings were usually constructed by craftspeople, highly skilled in their trades. This is how software development used to be: a single-profession task. Just as buildings are now the product of a collaboration between engineers, architects, and skilled tradespeople, so software development is becoming a collaborative process.

There will always be a place for effective one- or two-person organizations, combinations of extremely talented people who can both program and design successful, high-quality products, just as there are a few highly skilled carpenters who can do everything needed to remodel your house. But, more and more, as in many fields, successful software products are the result of a team effort between designers and developers. For a small company or a one-person development shop, this can mean forming teams in creative ways at different points in the process, much as today's building contractors bring in specialized subcontractors to complete particular parts of a construction project.

Design and Engineering

Despite the need for engineers and designers to work together, they often have conflicting goals; they use different processes and speak different languages, which can complicate a collaboration. The goal of the engineer is to complete a piece of code and get it running and free of bugs as quickly, efficiently, and elegantly as possible. Engineers enjoy solving a specific problem that enables a feature in the product, and they usually start from a specification and a programming architecture, and then move on to complete each piece. They make refinements to eliminate bugs, increase speed, or decrease the size of the code. Design of the algorithms and program architecture is a significant creative part of the early stage, when engineers often try out alternative strategies for solving problems.

Conversely, designers start with an idea to communicate. They produce multiple alternative designs, evaluate those designs, then redesign, reevaluate, and gradually arrive at the best solution. Along the way, they test with typical users, research alternative strategies, and factor in an accumulated knowledge of design history, fashion, and aesthetic sense to the solution. A talented designer quickly arrives at an elegant solution that communicates well, motivates, and is appealing. A talented programmer quickly arrives at an elegant solution that is efficient, bug-free, and fits seamlessly into the overall architecture. While both disciplines are required to build a successful product, generally the programmer's product interfaces with other computer programs, while the designer's product interfaces with people.

Goals conflict between designers and engineers when a good visual or functional design makes for slow or complex code. They conflict when the engineer doesn't understand the designer's iterative process, and wants to keep existing, working code in the product. They conflict when the most efficient code does not communicate well to the user. And perhaps worst of all, they disagree when, for example, the aesthetic taste of the engineer favors wild, exciting computer games, and the designer prefers the quiet subtlety of Shaker furniture. [figures 1.12 and 1.13]

Everyone Has an Opinion

Design is an art, and in art everyone has an opinion. Graphical software interfaces are used by millions of people every day, each of whom has an opinion about how good the interface is, how "user-friendly," how "intuitive," or how "attractive" it is. Not only do users have opinions, so do the product development team's colleagues, friends, marketing people, managers, support people, documentation writers, interface designers, and usability testers.

1.12 Too often, software development teams argue over differences in aesthetic taste. This game is visually powerful, and has an exciting design for a game, but it is not a good aesthetic model for office productivity software.

1.13 This room full of Shaker furniture is an example of the subtle, clean, and functional aesthetic that many designers aspire to emulate. Although this aesthetic suits office productivity software very well, it would be poorly suited to children's software or thrill-seeking games. Photo: Leo de Wys Inc./Grace Schaub.

As you work on your interface design, be prepared for an excess of opinions, and commit yourself to listen and stay open to suggestions, even though it will be difficult. You can't design for yourself, because you are never the typical user. You must investigate and weigh every suggestion, in an effort to produce the best product. This is how great products are made. If you rush your product to market with the best guess for an interface, using yourself as the model user, it will never be as good as it could have been, and sometimes it will be barely usable. Take the time to listen and redesign, and the result will be of higher quality.

Your goal is to design and create a simple yet powerful tool, where every detail has been deliberately drawn for smooth completion of the task. Imagine using a well-crafted hand tool; stop for a moment to admire how easily it fits in your hand, and how quickly and efficiently it accomplishes the task. This is just how your interface should feel. [figure 1.14]

1.14 Common hand tools have evolved over hundreds of years to fit both the task and size and shape of the human hand. Tools like this have had the advantage of many iterations to improve the nuances of their design. Photo: CMCD/Photodisk.

Design Roles Are Evolving

In every industrial field, tension exists between designers and engineers. But in more established fields, such as automobile manufacture or industrial product design, their roles are more clearly delineated. Software design still is a very young industry, and we are only beginning to determine everyone's roles. Because how something looks is apparent to everyone and the underlying code is not, it is easy to evaluate and criticize the interface design; it is more difficult to determine the strengths and weaknesses of the underlying code. (This is a fundamental difference between software design and other consumer product design fields: In most manufacturing processes, the engineer is not physically building the final product; for example, automobile engineers don't actually build the cars. But software programmers actually build the programming code.)

Nevertheless, software engineering teams that are used to having total control of their products can be persuaded to collaborate with visual designers when they realize the marketing value of good design. Certainly, they're as aware as everyone else that a more beautiful design will help sell the product, and it is always gratifying to see a product reach a wider market. [figure 1.15]

Windows Visual Interface Design

In this book, I will give you the information you need to build Windows software that is attractive to today's consumers. It is a compilation of the research I have done and the experience I have gained in seven years of designing the Windows interface. I have approached the topic so that it is of interest

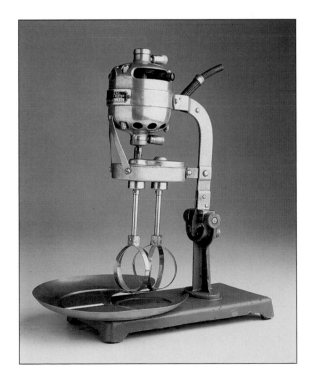

1.15 This mixer is the result of an early attempt at the design of a home mixer. Unfortunately, it resembles an industrial tool, not an appliance meant for the home. It may be well engineered, but because of its appearance, it was not successful. Photo: The Science Museum, Science & Society Picture Library, London, UK.

to both programmers and designers. To that end, I have tried to provide as many positive examples as I can, because although negative examples are easy to come by and have something to teach us, positive examples are more inspiring.

In this first part, I provide you with a broad foundation. I explain what design is and the effects of style; I describe the impact of design, the ideal design process, then detail a design strategy. In Part II, I condense a year-long graphic design course into two chapters, explaining the elements of graphic design using examples to illustrate how they apply to software interfaces. In Part III, I discuss the psychology of design, which is always an instrumental factor in the human-computer equation. I abbreviate a course on the psychology of perception, cultural differences, and explain the idea of affordance and how it relates to realism in the interface; then I talk about the unique problems of design for the screen. In Part IV, I get more specific about interface visuals concentrating on color, icons, and fonts. In Part V, I give advice, in the form of interface makeovers, examples of great interfaces, and advice about common pitfalls. Obviously, all of these topics could be treated in more depth, but my goal is to give you just enough information to inspire you to make better, more beautiful, Windows products.

2

The Effects of Visual Impact

Aesthetics: A Matter of Opinion and Taste

Design aesthetics are as diverse as people. Some favor orange shag carpets, others can abide only soft, thick, beige wall-to-wall; still others insist on hardwood floors accented by oriental rugs. What is good taste to some is boring to others. What is fun and exciting to some is overwhelming and ugly to others. Naturally, designers too debate the relative qualities and nuances of good design. Certainly, some kinds of taste are more widely recognized as "sophisticated," or at least are known to be more expensive. [figure 2.1] Other kinds of taste

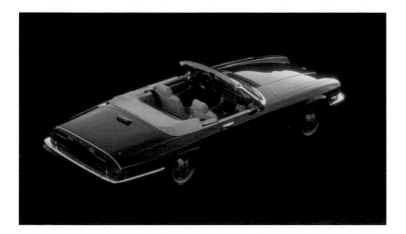

2.1 This car looks sophisticated, elegant, and expensive. An important early design decision is whether you want your product to have the metaphorical impact of a Jaguar or a Buick, of a minivan or a sport utility vehicle, of a Mercedes Benz or a Chevy Nova. Photo: Leo de Wys Inc./Rick Rusing.

may be considered old-fashioned, and still others childlike or cheap.

Imagine a Jaguar or a Mercedes alongside a Chevrolet or a Plymouth. You expect the more expensive car to have a lush interior, in soft, neutral colors, whereas you probably expect the cheaper car to have a vinyl interior, possibly in brighter colors.

Visuals influence communication for all of us, every day. We are assaulted by print and television advertisements, each designed to arouse a certain emotion and communicate a specific concept. The same principles that work in those ads should be working for you in your interface design.

Visuals Define Style

Just as in advertisements, color, typography, layout, and illustration arouse strong emotions and communicate subconscious messages to the user. These aesthetic choices determine the *style* of the interface. Colors convey feelings to such an extent that the disciplines of color science and psychology were developed to explain how and why. Typography can make text appear conservative and reliable or fashionably modern. Pictures or illustrations can be reassuring or shocking, sexy or bland.

So, aesthetic choices determine the style of a design and the style determines the customer's emotional reaction. Just as in a successful ad, an interface can seem engaging, playful, or provocative. Or as in an unsuccessful ad, it can be boring and uninteresting, or needlessly shocking.

In many interfaces, like Microsoft Bob, the cartoony illustrative style was a purposeful choice of the designers. In the Bob UI, very explicit ideas about a casual, user friendly appearance were designed and tested with home users. [figure 2.2] In some interfaces, however, design choices are made for

Rather than relying on personal taste in your design, pitch your aesthetic toward your audience. Ask yourself: What will the customer consider appropriate? What do you want to communicate to your customer about the value, sophistication, or reliability of your product? ▌▌

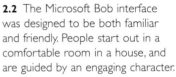

2.2 The Microsoft Bob interface was designed to be both familiar and friendly. People start out in a comfortable room in a house, and are guided by an engaging character.

engineering expedience or just arbitrarily. The result usually is an interface that elicits all the wrong subconscious emotional responses from the user. It has no distinct style, or an inconsistent and confusing one. Consequently, it may shout to the user: "This product is poor quality!" or "This product is very complicated!" or "This product is dull and boring!" It may make the user feel uncomfortable, confused, mystified, or even angry. [figure 2.3]

Visuals Affect Usability

In addition to eliciting emotional responses, visual design can also increase or decrease usability. If an interface is designed haphazardly, users won't know where to start or how to proceed. They won't know what's most important, and what is secondary, nor will they be able to find what they want in the melange of visual stimuli. Completing their task will become slow and annoying.

In designing your interface, you want to elicit positive emotions from your users. To do this, you need to use, for instance, subtle colors, clear arrangements, and unobtrusive visual cues to prompt a calm, comfortable response from an office worker; or use shocking colors, wild arrangements, and loud noises to get a game player excited about winning. ▌▌

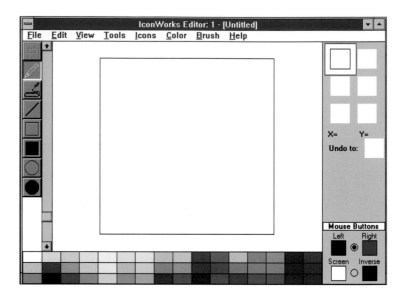

2.3 This interface is hard to understand. The tool buttons are difficult to discern: everything is big and in your face, but it's not clear what to do, or what is meant by the different visuals on the screen.

Mentally, we all rank the importance of information based on visual presentation, regardless of the medium. For example, in film, a well-constructed scene communicates clearly, and gently guides the viewer to look at the proper elements in a certain order. It should be obvious who the main characters are and who the extras are. In books, we use headlines, subheads, text columns, and figure captions to group and organize information.

In this same way, on a computer screen we need a mental path through the information. The most frequently performed functions should be the most obvious. [figure 2.4] Less frequently used functions, or expert features, should be progressively disclosed (initially hidden, but revealed at the right time). The most common task, like dialing a modem in communications software, should be the most obvious, and not buried in the middle of a list of menus. [figures 2.5 and 2.6]

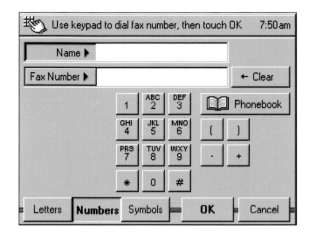

2.4 Although there are many controls on this small dialog, it is clear how to perform the most common task, because it is described at the top. Your attention is drawn to the instruction by the small graphic in the upper left-hand corner, which is the first place we usually look in Western societies, because we read left to right and top to bottom.

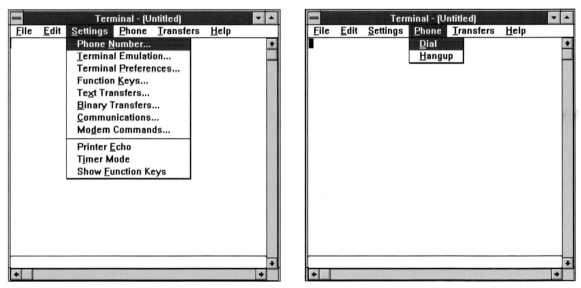

2.5 and **2.6** Although this was supposed to be a very simple modem program, the most common task occurs under the fourth menu item, after the very technically complex Settings menu. A better presentation would have the Dial function as the primary command, perhaps on a large graphic button, with File, Edit, Settings, and Transfer commands presented in a dialog, or as a setup wizard.

Clear Visuals Promote Efficiency

Clarity of presentation enables users to find what they want to complete the task at hand with the minimum of cognitive load. Clarity also promotes efficiency; less time is spent finding things or figuring things out. Finally, a clear design affects the bottom line, because a more efficient interface design means less training time. Most companies large and small diligently assess how much training will be needed before adopting new software. If your product can be shown to require little or no training time, it will be much more popular.

Visuals Affect Marketing and Marketing Affects Visuals

The marketing and visuals of a user interface form a symbiotic relationship. After all, before even beginning a design, you ask, who are the customers? What are their tastes and their expectations? Obviously there are big differences in the taste of and expectations between software engineers, kids, home users, and office workers. Engineers don't want an interface that is too childlike; they expect technical sophistication and don't want to be talked down to. [figure 2.7] Kids won't like an interface that is dry and technical; they're looking for bright colors, exciting activity, and engaging characters. [figure 2.8] Home users want to balance their computerized checkbook; they don't want to spend a lot of time figuring out how to use their software for such simple tasks. Office workers must be respected as professionals; usually, they are working in a more formal environment, and won't appreciate too many cute sounds or pictures; they need

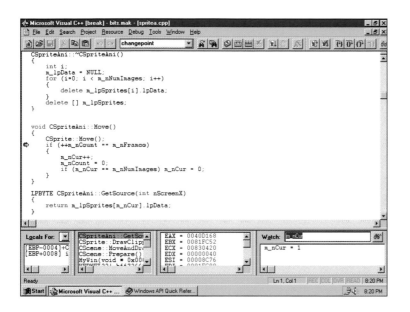

2.7 Microsoft Visual C++ is designed for maximum efficiency and customizability for the programmer. It has a straightforward functional interface with multiple small windows which can be positioned according to the user's preference. It also allows for extensive customization of colors and fonts.

2.8 Kid Pix by Brøderbund uses simple drawings and tools that small children can see and understand, even if they can't read.

sophisticated designs that are warm and inviting, clear and direct, which empower them to do their job. [figure 2.9]

A well-designed visual interface targets its audience from many vantage points: usability, tasks, features, and appearance. When an interface is put together without taking into account the aesthetic expectations of the audience, or without sufficient knowledge of how to meet those expectations, the effect can be damaging to the success of your product—indeed, your company. To avoid this unfortunate outcome, the designers and developers of the product must agree on a clear design strategy, before they start work on the product.

Well-designed interface elements are important selling features that distinguish a product from the competition. In the early '90s, Lotus used its consistent tool button graphics on all its advertising. In doing so, it was promoting a key feature of its products, while also showing off how visually sophisticated and friendly it was. By promoting its tool buttons, Lotus was saying that these products had been

2.9 Microsoft Word is designed to enable the office professional to be productive at a wide variety of word processing tasks.

designed by professionals for professionals: a very market-driven approach to product design. [figure 2.10]

Details Count

"God is in the details," said Mies Van Der Rohe, a famous architect and member of the Bauhaus, a German design school that developed many of today's theories of modernism in art, architecture, and design. In this famous quote, he meant that the beauty and richness of a building are in the details. When they are designed coherently, the myriad small details of a building combine to transcend the functional structure and bring the building to life. Not paying close attention to the details can result in an absence of aesthetic integration, a failure to create the most beautiful building possible.

The quote is probably a variation on the old German saying "the devil is in the details," an expression that meant that details were tricky and could trip you up, like the small print on a legal contract. "God is in the details" is a potent

2.10 The consistent, colorful toolbar graphics used in Lotus products were an important selling point when the product first shipped.

and positive reversal—the details are supreme, empowering. [figure 2.11]

Like a building, a user interface is more than the sum of its details, many of which are extremely subtle and often overlooked by software designers. Frequently, details are ignored to accommodate a shorter development schedule, or, worse, because someone thinks they are unimportant. But every tiny detail counts. Weigh design trade-offs with care, because each detail purposefully designed and integrated with the whole leads to a clarity of presentation and function. [figure 2.12]

Quantifying Talent and Taste

Neither architecture nor software product design are exact sciences because they deal with two hard to quantify variables: human psychology and aesthetic taste. And two

2.11 The unique character of each building is more than the sum of its details.

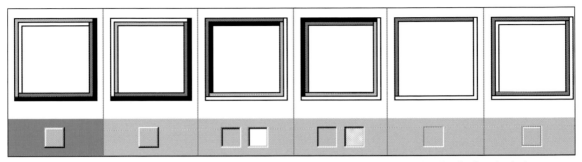

2.12 The design of 3-D elements in Windows 95 was created with close attention to the detail of each pixel.

elements of those variables—talent and intuition—can be frustrating to engineers who are used to being able to measure results. Design is hard if not impossible to quantify, and therefore it is difficult to gauge its success, although usability testing and focus groups do provide some hard data.

Usability tests are based on the methods of experimental psychology; they examine users' interaction with software, in an effort to discover what's easy, what's hard, what works, and what doesn't. Focus groups are a classic marketing method, in which a small group of potential customers are asked for their reactions to product ideas.

Usability testing is an excellent method for determining which features of a product work. It provides a means for finding out how software functionality is understood by actual users, which enables both engineers and designers to improve the features and interactive design of a product. But these tests are inexact—they assess only part of the user experience, because they are given in an unnatural environment such as a testing lab, and therefore can evaluate only segments of the product. To gather data about the entire product in actual use, a long field study is required; unfortunately, field studies seldom gauge emotional response.

Focus groups help get a sense of how people feel and what they'll buy, but, again, because of the artificial nature of the groups, the data is only partially reliable. Focus groups and usability testing alone won't create an excellent product: talent, good judgment, intuition, skill, and artistry are all needed to produce a great interface.

The visual design of a Windows software interface, even if it closely follows the standard guidelines, will always have an impact on the usability and marketability of the program. The more attention paid to the visual style and the details of the visual presentation, the more usable and successful the product will be for its target audience.

3

The Process for Designing Visual Interfaces

Visual design is integral to the whole development process, and therefore should be considered elemental right from the beginning. You can't write your spec, write your code, and then add some good design at the end. Once the spec is complete and the code is written, you can't easily change the presentation of information, except in very minor ways. Therefore, you must *start* with the vision for the graphic presentation and user interactions, then develop the functional spec in conjunction with its image. At the outset, draw a broad outline of your features, determine who your target market audience is, and define a style. Next, draw a variety of prototype ideas. Probably the biggest mistake most software companies make is to either do no prototyping at all, or do it without involving someone trained in the aesthetics of product or graphic design. [figure 3.1]

The Ideal Team

There are many ways to form a software design team. The specific roles of the individuals will vary, of course, depending on their talents and expertise and the requirements of the project. But the ideal team should include professionals with expertise in each of the following areas:

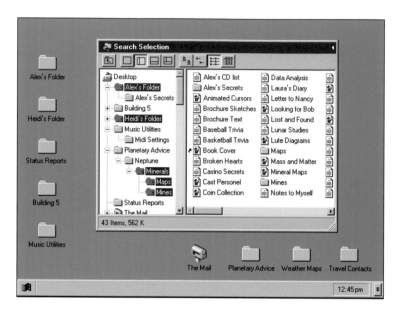

3.1 This was a very early prototype of Windows 95. Visual designers worked as integral members of the team years before Windows 95 shipped.

- software design engineering
- functional spec design
- visual interface design
- prototyping
- usability testing
- marketing
- writing

And the specific titles used to identify these roles may be different: programmer, user interface designer, graphic designer, human factors specialist, documentation writer. A large team may be made up of several people with each skill set, whereas a small team may have one person who fills two or three of these roles. Some products may even be developed by only one person who designs the interface, writes the code, tests the code, usability tests with users, and writes and designs the documentation. Often a team will hire contractors for parts of the process. The key is not how many or what they're called; the key is to be sure to include the right skill sets at the right time. Each of these hats *must* be worn by someone, so that all bases are covered. [figure 3.2] Every developer should have at least a part-time graphic or product designer to help the visualization of the user interface to unfold. To repeat, this designer should be involved from the beginning, when a greater, more far-reaching, impact can be made.

The Ideal User Interface Design Process

The following steps detail an ideal process for designing an interface. Every team, no matter how small, should touch on every step during product development.

1. *Contextual inquiry:* This is the starting place for user-centered design. Contextual inquiry is based on anthropological techniques for studying a culture and gathering data about it. In terms of software, it means spending time with the users and observing them. You simply watch them and take extensive notes, while considering these questions: How do they do

3.2 There are many functional roles in a software project; the visual interface design hat is just one. Photo: Planet Art.

their current tasks? What are blocks to their efficiency? How could software improve their work? What are the conceptual paradigms that they understand? How do they structure their tasks? What are familiar names and ideas?

2. *Design and prototype:* Once user data has been collected, evaluate it to help you identify the tasks users need to accomplish and the features you want to implement to make it easier for them. Then begin the design of those features, paying close attention to the notes you took about the way people work, the visual cues they understand, and the language that they use. Decide on a design strategy and a visual style.

   Once you feel sure that your early designs address these issues, prototype those features, first in drawings with explanatory text, and later with quick-running prototypes of parts of the user interface. Initially, the drawings can be pencil and paper, then more detailed bitmaps. But one word of caution: you should never just write a verbal spec—remember, this is a graphical interface! Paper prototypes are excellent starting points only; it is very important to put the parts together on the screen and see the interface in motion. Like an animated film, many of the details of an interface come to life when they move and interact.

3. *Usability test:* Test the prototypes with users. Even if all you have are paper prototypes, you can get helpful data by asking users to try to complete a task using pictures that step them through each stage. At this juncture, you can also conduct focus groups to test the

market. The information you get from these groups tends to be less concrete but still very useful. It's important to realize that you don't need a laboratory or professionally designed tests to get data from users. There are many informal methods for quick usability testing, and any information you get from real users trying your product is better than none. Of course, if you can do formal usability tests, so much the better; in which case, do as many as you can—the power and value of usability data is incalculable. (Refer to books in the reference section for information on usability testing methods.)

4. *Iterate:* Refine your design based on usability and focus group data, then retest. Continue redesigning and retesting until the design works with users. If you are part of a small team and don't have the resources to do actual usability tests or running prototypes, it is nevertheless important that you visualize the design with drawings of screens and dialogs. Even during the drawing process, flaws in the feature design or interaction model will emerge, and your product designer can then generate ideas to improve the graphic presentation.

5. *Develop:* Only after you have done several iterations of a user interface design should you start writing code. The code should be based on the prototypes and be usability-tested again as soon as pieces of the code are running.

6. *Polish:* Once the code is in place, polish and tune the interface. The visual interface designer should review all the dialogs, checking them against dialog layout standards for spacing and alignment. The writer

should check and correct all text usage. The designer should create all the window and tool icons and any dialog bitmaps or animations that will aid in usability. Lastly, complete the product icon, the opening screen, and other marketing-driven graphic elements.

Through the Designer's Eyes

As just illustrated, the complete user interface design process involves a team and several steps, with visual issues affecting the development process at every stage. But software product design as seen through the eyes of the visual designer provides another vantage point of the design process.

Creativity

For the designer, the early stages of a project are the most creative. Working with the developers and other team members, visual interface designers draw sketches of ideas and make running prototypes in programs such as Visual Basic or Macromind Director. Most designers start with a strategy based on their knowledge of the market for the product; they next ask team members and management to agree on a visual style before advancing to in-depth drawings. (More on design strategy in the next chapter.)

Many Windows products, especially those created for an office environment, use the Windows 95 interface guidelines and standard system controls, where many of the design elements are defined. Nevertheless, there is still a wide latitude for creativity. When the product must appeal to more of a home audience, the style may be more similar to that for the multimedia CD market, and this will define both the interaction and presentation style. The colors and fonts available, along with the development time and memory restrictions, will also help define the style of the product.

Designers start with hand-drawn paper sketches of ideas, [figure 3.3] or collages made up of pieces from existing products, they want to emulate. They look at how these ideas can be adapted to the new product, then consider what new ideas are needed. After sketching many ideas and trying numerous alternatives, they move to on-screen drawings and running prototypes.

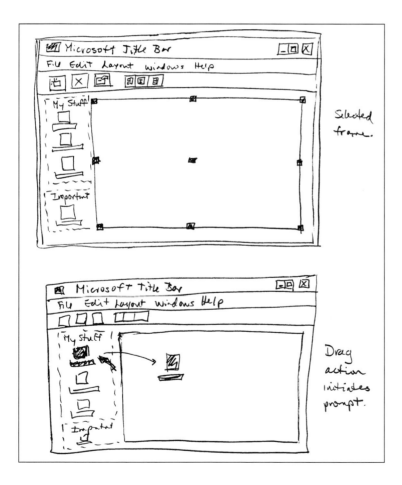

3.3 Many designers begin their prototypes by drawing quick sketches. These sketches allow them to quickly work out key interface elements and interactions, before drawing detailed bitmaps on the screen.

Production

Once the design is fairly well defined and code is being written, the designer goes into production mode. This is the time to do those exacting grids for alignment of controls, and to tweak all the details of animation, sound, graphics, and typography. In the real world and rapid pace of software schedules, design and production stages may overlap. But attention to detail in the production stage should be near and dear to the heart of any designer.

Review and Polish

As the product gets to an alpha stage, it's critical for designers to review the running code and look for visual bugs, such as misalignments, control sizing and spacing, colors and animations. As when testing the code for functional bugs, it's important to have several visual reviews.

Finally, the last details are applied, like the pinstripes on a car—the spit and polish. The final icons and graphics are added and refined, the start-up screens are completed, and the product is ready for the world.

4

Developing a Visual Interface Design Strategy

The major factors that the design team must address early in the conceptual process for a software product are audience expectations, technical considerations, schedule and resources, and the competition. The decisions the team makes regarding these factors define the entire project and serve as the basis for a design strategy. They have a dramatic effect on the visual presentation and must be evaluated and integrated early in the development process. These decisions will subsequently determine many of the numerous details of the interface as it comes together over time. Teams often skip this key stage and rush into doing prototypes. The result is a lot of wasted effort. Without a clearly defined design strategy, you'll end up redesigning and starting over many times.

A design strategy can also serve as an effective way of bringing the team together behind a common goal. The strategy can be a formal written document, or the result of team brainstorming. Whoever is assuming the visual design role for the product should be the steward of the design strategy, keeping notes and making sure that all team members agree to it before development begins.

Audience Expectations

Naturally, your major consideration is your audience, both in terms of functional expectations and visual presentation. What does your audience expect and how can you deliver it to them?

Consistency with the Operating System

Be consistent with the aesthetic ideas embodied in the visual details of the various operating systems (Windows NT 3.51 and Windows 3.1 vs. Windows 95); don't mix them together into strange hybrids. ▎▊

The first big decision you make is whether your product will follow Windows 95 interface guidelines and use Windows controls. If you are designing a business application, consistency with the operating system is essential. The more your user interface applies Windows user interface standards, the more users will be able to transfer what they have learned in other programs to yours. Consistency with Windows guidelines also means less training time, as well as greater ease of learning and ease of use. [figure 4.1] Windows 95 has a fairly stringent set of guidelines that must be implemented properly in order for a product to be labeled as Windows 95-compatible, with the Windows 95 logo on the box. (See the Windows 95 interface style guide: *The Windows Interface*

4.1 For many productivity applications, consistency with the operating system is the first essential element of the design strategy. Microsoft WordPad is a small application that applies the interface standards consistently by using standard controls and arrangements.

Guidelines for Software Design, published by Microsoft Press, for detailed information.)

If your product is a multimedia title or an Internet title, the audience will expect more visual excitement than you can get with the standard controls. But it is still important to know the guidelines. You need to be aware of the common controls and interactions users are already familiar with. In the traditional graphic design world, setting up consistent rules and then choosing just the right moment to break them creates suspense, surprise, and drama. The same is true of interface design, as long as you never lose sight of the product's purpose. A multimedia title is like a book, which is usually read once or twice; therefore, it can afford to be lively and unusual, as long as it is coherent. Conversely, a productivity application that will be used for hours every day should be more standardized and unobtrusive.

Style

In terms of visual presentation, style is the next big decision. Styles are aesthetic, often emotionally generated, and go in and out of fashion. If you want a product with a timeless design, think classical. Classic designs are usually sophisticated, clear, and understated. They can be analogized to Shaker furniture or coffee table books. [figure 4.2] If your product is trendy, you can afford to go for something wild and wacky, in which case, think toys and games. [figure 4.3]

There are innumerable variations on style, and sometimes it is easier to describe when comparing extremes, such as business software versus childrens' products, but even minor variations in an interface that uses standard controls can create an individual sense of style. A classic style in a standard interface would have every element aligned, spaced

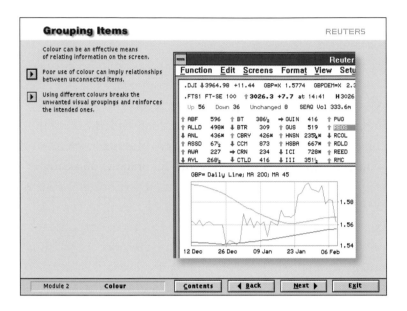

4.2 This interface design tutorial by Reuters has a clear, professional aesthetic. It is simple, but with enough subtle details to add interest. Designed by Rodney Edwards of interAction graphics for Reuters, Ltd.

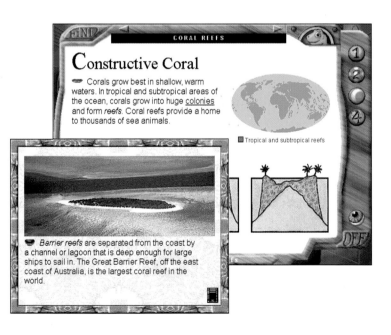

4.3 Microsoft Explorapedia uses colored borders, curved edges, textures, and quirky animating controls to hold the interest of small children.

and placed evenly; there would be only a few graphics, in black and white or muted colors; there would be nothing extraneous in the design anywhere. A flashier design using standard controls could easily look out of control. But, if done with attention to detail, using, for example, a specific and consistent dialog layout scheme that broke the standard rules, it could nonetheless be clear and effective. It perhaps would incorporate larger, more colorful graphics and titles in nonstandard fonts, illustrations, wizards, and textures—but in well-thought out and consistent ways.

It is usually easier to create classic style designs, because they don't push the boundaries and they rely on clarity and simplicity to work. There are also more models to emulate and arriving at a design just takes diligent attention to detail. Flashier designs are harder to make effective, because they involve more artistry and require achieving a delicate balance of rules followed and rules broken.

Functions

In terms of functional expectations, the controls you use should match your audience. Your product has to be designed to communicate a specific type of information (such as a multimedia title) or to reach a unique audience (say, children). Sometimes a slight modification of Windows controls will work. [figure 4.4] Or you may use some of the Windows interactions, but accomplish other aspects of the interface with arrows, comic characters, sounds, or other cues. [figure 4.5]

Communication Design Principles and Psychology

When you design and implement a Windows interface, you are doing both graphic and communication design. Graphic design motivates, communicates, clarifies, and inspires

4.4 Microsoft Multimedia Mozart uses buttons that look like Windows controls, but in a softer color. This is one simple variation from the operating system's visuals.

4.5 Microsoft Magic School Bus uses large pictorial symbols and a talking lizard character for navigational controls. It makes sense to use nonstandard controls in this product for small children.

confidence. Communication principles differ from style or consistency with standards; they feed into both of these, but involve what the user understands, as well as what he or she feels. So, in addition to the tasks you want to support with features and the style of your design, you need to define as part of your design strategy how you will communicate with your users.

Most productivity software strives for clear communication—the user should feel in control and not talked down to or patronized. To achieve a communication style, the visual design must create a synergy with the writing style of text as well as with the sequence of controls and the breakdown of tasks.

Technical Considerations

Technical constraints including colors, fonts, memory, and disk space all affect the scope of a design. A creative designer can do an excellent design with limited resources, but he or she cannot achieve anything unless the design parameters are established. These technical constraints will also become part of the design strategy. The design strategy may be based on how to take advantage of the advanced technical features of the product; on the other hand, it may be based on how to work around technical limitations. Either way, all the technical parameters of the product have to be discussed and agreed on *before* the design process starts. [figure 4.6]

Schedule and Resources

Schedule is of course an important factor in any design strategy. There will always be trade-offs between product features and the schedule. The designer may have wonderful

4.6 Microsoft Dangerous Creatures was developed with very limited resources. There was no development time for fancy animations, so instead photographs were used that went to the edges of the screen. These large, colorful pictures became the theme of the product, with other elements layered over them, and the animations were not missed.

A word of warning: Don't ever copy another product's good design, and don't steal icons or graphic elements from other products. Icons and graphics are copyrighted, and infringing someone's copyright is unwise, to say the least. ▍▍

ideas, but if they can't be programmed in time, they won't end up in the final product. Part of the design strategy should be a determination of which design elements are high priorities and which are less important. Sometimes a design is evolutionary; that is, part of the design elements are included in the first release, and the rest go into the next release.

A short schedule and limited resources should never be an excuse for a boring design. It's very important to start every design with a sky's-the-limit approach, or you'll miss discovering good ideas, even when you scale back. It is always easier to refine and reduce an elaborate design than to inflate a minimalist one.

The Competition

Needless to say, it's important to know your competition. Be sure to evaluate not only their strengths and weaknesses in terms of features and marketing, but also in terms of design. Ask yourself: Can you create a design that will better address the needs of the user, and thereby gain market share? And don't forget to consider other products that are not direct competition. How effective are the design strategies of products you admire?

Conclusion

You build a design strategy based on your priorities for the user, the market and audience, the competition, your preferred style, and possible consistency with the operating system or other software. In your design strategy, you make use of communication principles and marketing data, and you plan for prototyping and usability testing. With a clear design strategy as your base, it's much easier to work out the details of the product design as it evolves.

Part Two

Graphic Design Principles

5

Universal Design Principles

The Art of Design

Currently, it is not fashionable to acknowledge the importance of talent in design. Many would have design be something quantifiable, rational, scientific. And while good design does yield quantifiable results in improved usability, and the psychological aspects of design may be isolated and tested for their "human factors," some aspects of design elude analysis. As in art criticism, it is difficult to verbally describe visual impact. [figures 5.1 and 5.2]

To design is much more than simply to assemble, to order, or even to edit; it is to add value and meaning, to illuminate, to simplify, to clarify, to modify, to dignify, to dramatize, to persuade, perhaps even to amuse. To design is to transform prose into poetry. Design broadens perception, magnifies experience, enhances vision. Design is the product of feeling and awareness, of ideas that originate in the mind of the designer and culminate, one hopes, in the mind of the spectator.

—Paul Rand, in *Design Form and Chaos*

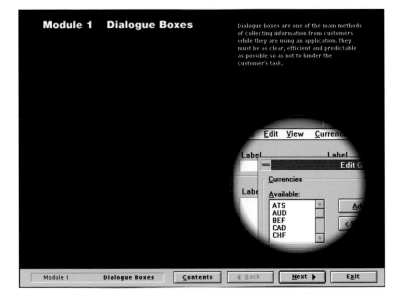

5.1 In this training module, Reuters uses a classic style of graphic design to communicate good design principles for its Windows products. Designed by Rodney Edwards of interAction graphics for Reuters, Ltd.

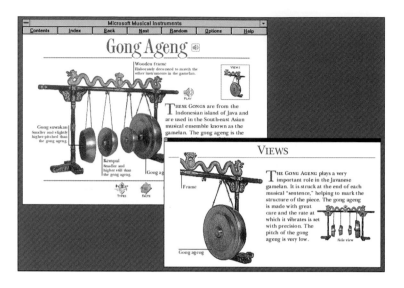

5.2 The generous white background and classic serif typefaces, as well as the elegant compositions, make Microsoft Musical Instruments a classic, timeless design.

There are many principles that define aesthetic choice, most of which are complex, subtle, and confined to the philosophy of art. Some designers like to refer to semiotics (the philosophy of signs and symbols), which was in vogue in the conceptual art of the 1970s. But there is more to design than semiotics or other visual philosophies. Essentially, design is the art of defining form. The aesthetic element of defining form always involves taste and talent, but there are a few fundamental principles that anyone can use to improve a design.

Fundamental Principles of Design

Beauty, defined in the preceding quote by Paul Rand in his book *Design Form and Chaos* as one half of the "good design accolade," is hard to describe and is most often arrived at through intuition. As I mentioned earlier, taste is "in the eye of the beholder"; aesthetic judgment is personal and emotional. But throughout human history and across many cultures, a small number of universal aesthetic principles have emerged. These are broad qualities that most professionals agree constitute excellence in art and design. [figure 5.3]

To develop graphic design fluency with these aesthetic principles requires spending several years in a professional graphic design school, but I will briefly describe the most basic principles here, in the context of interface design. These descriptions will do two things: they will help you to understand how designers make design choices, and they will improve the aesthetic choices you make in your own day-to-day work on software. The three general design principles I will describe are harmony, balance, and simplicity. These can best be achieved using a few simple methods: refinement, restraint, unity, and modularity.

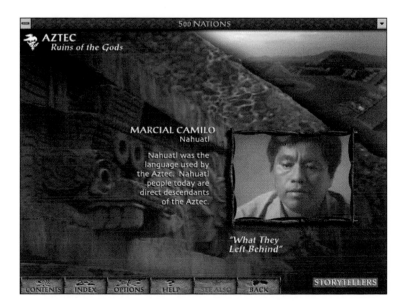

Many designers, schooled or self-taught, are interested primarily in things that look good and work well; they see their mission realized only when aesthetics and practical needs coalesce. What a designer does is not limited to any particular idea or form. Graphic design embraces every kind of problem of visual communication, from birth announcements to billboards. It embodies visual ideas, from the typography of a Shakespearean sonnet to the design and typography of a box of Kellogg's Corn Flakes. What might entitle these items to the good design accolade is their practicability and their beauty, both of which are embodied in the idea of quality.

—Paul Rand, in Design Form and Chaos

5.3 The CD title Microsoft 500 Nations is an excellent design: beautiful, clear, and engaging, while remaining quietly respectful of the content of the title.

Harmony

Harmony is probably the most important design principle when applied to software interfaces. Design harmony is achieved when all the elements of an interface fit together seamlessly; when movement from one element to another is effortlessly smooth; when the configuration of every perceived element, whether visual, auditory, or functional, blends into a pleasing, satisfying whole. The most widely used example of harmony is Greek architecture, especially the golden rectangle. The Greeks developed elaborate mathematical canons relating the relative proportions of building elements to achieve the most aesthetically pleasing result. [figure 5.4]

Harmony affects even the smallest visual relationships. When each detail is designed to relate proportionally, the result is a pleasing form. In an interface, this is embodied in the layout of dialogs and all screen elements, but it also includes the style and sizes of elements, the sequencing of information, and feedback from the program to the user. An interface is harmonious when nothing seems out of place, no

5.4 Intricate proportional relationships formed the basis of both Greek architecture and mathematics. This picture of the Parthenon, from Microsoft Ancient Lands, reminds us that harmony of the parts to the whole has been an aesthetic tenet of Western society for thousands of years.

one feature is glaring or awkward, there are no surprises;
everything fits its purpose, one task leads pleasantly and
easily to the next, each large and small element is considered
and delicately integrated with the whole. Because graphical
user interface design is in its very early stages, very few
products have truly harmonious interfaces. But harmony
should be the first goal of a great user interface. [figure 5.5]

Balance

Balance, like harmony, relates to integrating elements, but it
refers more directly to arrangement. Artists and designers
always seek balance in a composition. Symmetry is the
simplest way of achieving balance, and it works in many
graphic design compositions. But symmetry can be very
limiting and therefore can easily become dull. The Greeks
used the principle of dynamic symmetry where carefully
computed complex mathematical proportions and

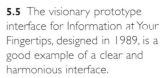

5.5 The visionary prototype interface for Information at Your Fingertips, designed in 1989, is a good example of a clear and harmonious interface.

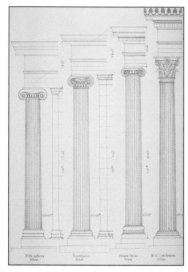

5.6 These Greek columns are one example of the principle of dynamic symmetry. Photo: Planet Art.

5.7 This cover of the *Quarter Point* newsletter from Monotype Typography has a complex asymmetrical composition, grounded on the subtle, black-shadowed M. The large M helps pull together elements on the top of the page, while the vertical alignment of the small rectangles unifies the gray top and red bottom of the page. Photo courtesy of Monotype Typography Inc.

relationships created a dynamism, a feeling of activity, that animated symmetrical arrangements. [figure 5.6]

Modern artists, architects, and designers generally prefer to achieve balance more through the heady challenge of *asymmetry*. Like a balance beam with unequal weights on the ends, modern compositions juxtapose large elements with small ones. Some elements are visually "heavier" than others—they are larger, darker, more brightly colored, more intricately detailed. This type of arrangement must be carefully worked out to achieve visual balance. [figure 5.7]

In an interface, balance is frequently a layout problem. Most often it involves the arrangement of elements on a screen, or of controls and graphics in a dialog. Screens and

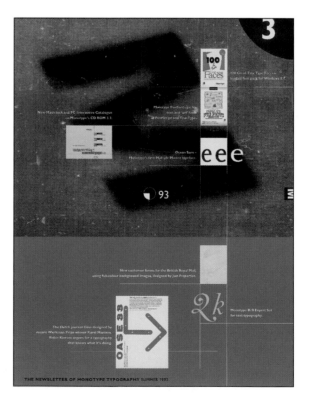

dialogs are usually asymmetrical compositions, which makes balance especially important. [figures 5.8 and 5.9] Occasionally, a roughly symmetrical dialog can be worked out where the axis of symmetry is centered vertically in the dialog. [figure 5.10] Rarely can a dialog be balanced with a horizontal axis of symmetry, where the top and bottom halves of a dialog mirror each other. Sometimes, a rough symmetry can be

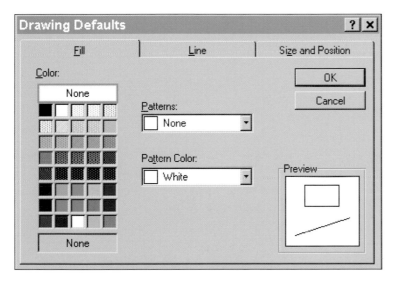

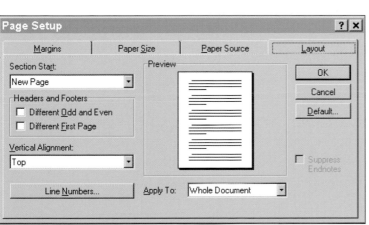

5.8 This dialog, from Microsoft Word, is not completely unbalanced but it looks haphazard. The controls are stuck in the four corners, and have no clear relationship to each other. A trick that designers use to see the balance of a composition is to squint their eyes. Try it now: squint your eyes until you can't see any of the details of the page in front of you. What you will see is dark and light shapes on the page. If all the dark areas are on one side, then the composition is out of balance.

5.9 This dialog, also from Microsoft Word, is not symmetrical, but it's nicely balanced. The controls seem to fall neatly into three columns.

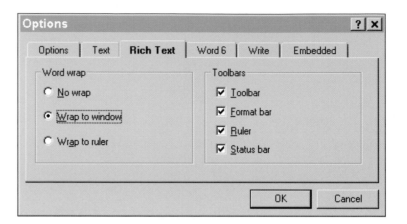

5.10 This dialog, from WordPad, is roughly symmetrical left to right, because of the two central group boxes. The buttons on the bottom right visually offset the title text in the upper left, creating a highly balanced composition.

> . . . *simplicity in design depends on three closely related principles. The elements in the design must be* unified *to produce a coherent whole, the parts (as well as the whole) must be* refined *to focus the viewer's attention on their essential aspects, and the fitness of the solution to the communication problem must be* ensured *at every level.*
>
> **Kevin Mullet and Darrel Sano, in**
> **Designing Visual Interfaces**

achieved with a diagonal axis, but by far the most common case is a struggle to integrate a number of very different elements into an asymmetrically balanced composition.

Simplicity

Simplicity, in the design sense, is not the reverse of complexity. Simple does not mean dull, dreary, or plain. Very complex patterns can be simple if they are balanced and harmonious. Simplicity in the context of design means clarity, sophistication, elegance, economy. Simplicity is direct, restrained, and subdued, yet full of nuance and meaning. The best examples of simplicity are of course found everywhere in nature, in the perfect form of a leaf, the amazing detail of a fractal, the quiet beauty of a snowflake. [figure 5.11]

A simple and elegant solution is a sought-after quality in mathematics, just as it is in design. And, as in math, the simple solution seems obvious once you arrive at it, but usually takes a long time or an exceptional talent to discover. In my experience with interface design, simplicity is achieved only through many iterations—designs and redesigns, refining, questioning, and testing all the way. [figure 5.12]

5.11 The beauty of a leaf is simple and elegant, and yet it has a complex structure. Photo: Leo de Wys Inc./Henryk T. Kaiser.

5.12 The main screen from Microsoft Multimedia Schubert, designed by the Voyager Company, has a simple symmetrical composition, and yet appears elegantly understated because of the water-covered stones in the background and the classic typeface.

In their book *Designing Visual Interfaces,* Kevin Mullet and Darrell Sano describe simplicity as the single most important quality of a good design.

Design Methods

Designers use a wide variety of methods to arrive at a harmonious solution. What follows are a few of the most common ones.

Refinement

Refinement is both a description of elegant sophistication and the best method through which to achieve it. The term "refinement" means the process of polishing, and in graphic design it is a method for achieving simplicity and harmony. You begin with a problem and try alternative methods to solve it; then you evaluate the results of the alternatives and refine them. You examine every element to identify places where you can reduce complexity, always striving to isolate the clearest, most succinct expression, and eliminate anything that does not contribute to that expression.

Restraint

Another method by which to achieve a simple design is restraint. Restraint may be regarded as a kind of "before-the-fact" refinement. Japanese design, art, and architecture are excellent examples of restraint. An elegant solution is arrived at by using the absolute minimum of elements, which are simply and artfully arranged to give an impression of quiet, understated sophistication. [figure 5.13]

5.13 This utilitarian Japanese object has a sculptural quality because of the large curves of the handles and the proportion of handles to blades. It is an extremely simple, restrained design with a timeless quality. Photo: CMCD/Photodisk.

Restraint, in the Japanese sense, does not apply to all interface designs. Some products are meant for a more casual or more exuberant market (like kids' games), but restraint still should be a guiding principle to apply in every stage of interface design. Even if you are working on a mass market product, it will benefit from eliminating extraneous elements, from holding back on that extra, seldom-needed feature. Restraint is the one design method which all software designers and programmers should use more often.

Unity

Unity simply means to combine or connect all the elements. A unified composition is inherently balanced and harmonious, so if you know you want things balanced, work on unifying them, and balance will certainly result. There are many ways to create unity: you can make things the same

5.14 This screen design from a Reuters tutorial exemplifies the graphic design principle of unity. It uses alignment in a two-column layout, and repetition of elements such as the arrow buttons, to create a regularized, unified feeling. Designed by Rodney Edwards of interAction graphics for Reuters, Ltd.

size or shape, align them or regularize them. [figure 5.14] You can arrange them so that one element appears to merge into the next, a visual phenomenon called closure. You can also use repetition to create a feeling of unity.

Modularity

Another method for achieving balance is through modularity. Modules are elements that are the same size, shape, and proportion. Frequently, they are created by breaking information into chunks, and then regularizing the pieces; the proportional elements then all fit together, like a puzzle. [figure 5.15]

The designer's grid grew out of attempts to modularize print graphic design. Grids are formal page layout designs, used in all the printed publications you see. They are

To achieve unity and balance in your interface, divide and arrange your elements into modules. Modules can help you achieve design balance through repetition, but be careful to vary some details for the sake of visual interest; strict modularity can be boring. Modules also help you to "chunk" your information, making it more accessible to the user. ▌▌

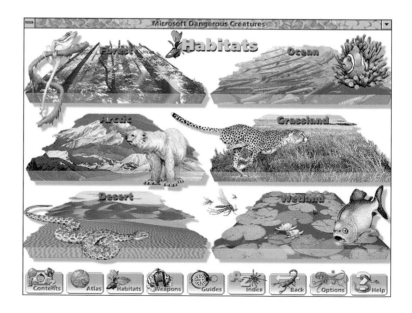

5.15 This screen, from Microsoft Dangerous Creatures, has a fairly symmetrical arrangement because of the six modules. Notice how the size and shape of the tilted landscapes are repeated, each with a headline of similar size. But there is variation in the placement of the animals on each landscape, which adds interest, along with differences in color and texture between the modules.

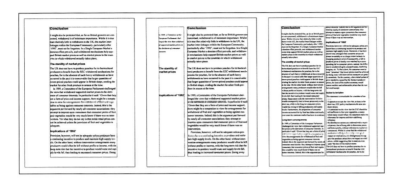

5.16 These three simple arrangements show how the grid allows you to create modules of text in a printed document. Illustration courtesy of *Designing Business Documents* by Monotype Typography Inc.

generally thought of as arrangements of columns, but they also include margins, white space, and graphics. Grids form the basis for the style of a printed document; raw text and graphics are modularized in them to become a coherent arrangement. The grid creates alignments, visual blocks, and a natural balance. [figures 5.16 and 5.17]

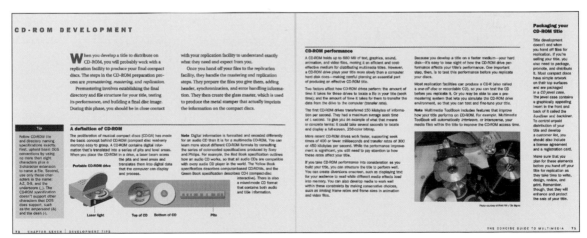

5.17 These pages from a manual on interactive design by Assymetrix Corporation show a typical two-column grid design with sidebars and illustrations. Design by Aliza Corrado

6

Graphic Information Design Principles

Graphic designers employ a large number of visual tools and techniques in their quest for a practical and beautiful design. These concepts are the direct application of the design principles and methods described in Chapter 5. It is somewhat difficult to pinpoint exactly how and why they work, because the same techniques used by different designers will yield different results.

Graphic design tools are properties of design elements (qualities of line, shape, type, or controls) which can be adjusted, or which are predefined and must be worked around. Techniques are generally methods that can be used to create a certain impact on the finished design. But there is a lot of overlap; tools and techniques are used together and influence each other.

Scale, contrast, and proportion are powerful tools in the hands of an experienced designer. If proportion sets the rhythm of the display, then the scale of its components determines its forcefulness, and their contrasts determine its excitability. These powerful elements must be used with care, particularly in interface design, where the goal is rarely to shock, to arrest, or to persuade. Contrasts must be clear enough to convey the intended distinctions, yet subtle enough to produce a harmonious relation between the elements in the display.

—Kevin Mullet and Darrell Sano, in *Designing Visual Interfaces*

Graphic Design Tools

The following design "tools" are elements of a design, or properties of elements. They can be varied to create different visual effects.

Scale

Scale refers to the proportion between two or more sets of dimensions, that is, sizes. Some elements are larger, some are

65

smaller. Large elements generally carry weight and convey strength, small elements usually are lighter and of less magnitude. Scale is relative because the size of something is usually seen in relation to the sizes of the things around it. [figure 6.2] Scaling elements in a design can generate a feeling

6.1 Designers use many computer software tools, but nothing beats the pencil for quick brainstorming and sketching. Photo: CMCD/ Photodisk.

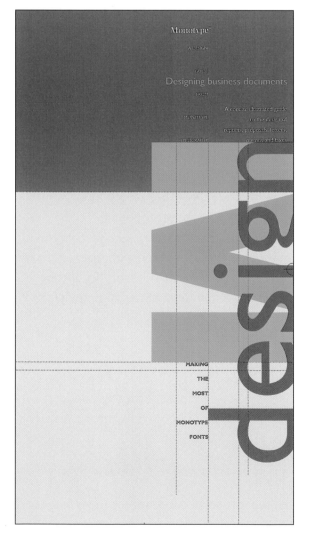

6.2 This brochure cover uses dramatic differences in scale to create an interesting design. Photo courtesy Monotype Typography Inc.

of depth; scaling can also imply relative importance, with larger things seeming more important than smaller ones.

Proportion

Proportion is the harmonious relation of one part of an element to another. Proportional relationships can be minutely ordered, as in Greek architecture, or they can be rough measurements. The proportional sizes and arrangement of elements determine the underlying structure of a design. The visual impact depends upon the size and proportion of every piece: Changing proportions changes the fundamental design. [figure 6.3]

Contrast

Contrast is the juxtaposition of dissimilar elements. You can use contrasting colors (black/white), contrasting shapes

6.3 In this screen from Microsoft Musical Instruments, the pictures in "The Families of Instruments" are all the same size. This creates a sense that they are of equal importance, in addition to setting up a simple, balanced layout. In "The Keyboard Family," the instrument pictures vary in size, according to the relative proportions of the actual, physical instruments.

(circles/squares), contrasting sizes (large/small), or contrasting values (light/dark). Contrast has a strong emotional component, and can be the force behind a dynamic display or a dull one. Good contrasts that are intentional but not overdone create liveliness. [figure 6.4] Too little contrast is boring and undistinguished. [figure 6.5] Too much contrast is distracting and overwhelming. Contrast, say, between the textures of leather and chrome in a chair, can be rich and delightful, yet subtle. Well-designed contrasts are the chocolate decadence of design.

Color

The use of color can create a powerful emotional force. Color trends in fashion prove how powerfully motivating color can be to human beings. Color is used throughout the world to indicate danger, caution, and comfort. It is intimately linked

Colors in vogue in the user interfaces of the 1990s are soft and neutral for professional applications, and wildly bright in games or applications that are trendy. ▌▌

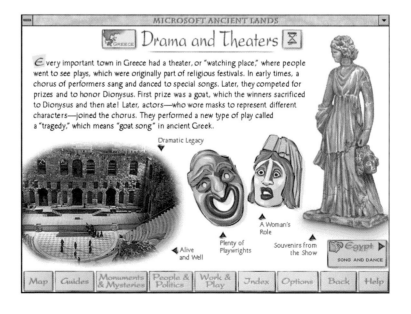

6.4 There are a number of interesting contrasts on this screen from Microsoft Ancient Lands, such as the photograph of the Greek theater with the hand-drawn illustrations of the masks and the statue.

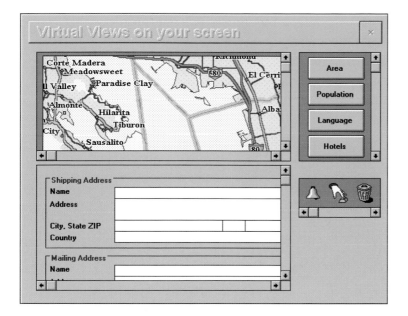

6.5 This application has far too little contrast in the title bar text, making it hard to read. This use of 3-D is not legible and it's not very interesting to look at, because it lacks contrast.

to important personal and cultural events including weddings, funerals, and religious festivals. Specific colors and color contrasts can be used to communicate as well as to attract attention. To use color successfully, however, style and fashion must be taken into account. For example, in the 1990s, no one would be caught dead with the avocado green refrigerators and orange shag carpets of the 1960s. [figure 6.6] Color is probably the most powerful design tool for aesthetic decision making, and, therefore, the details of color perception will be covered separately, later in the book. For now, remember that there is an aesthetic as well as a perceptual side to color.

Fonts

Typography is a well-established design discipline that is also highly subject to fashion. Fonts communicate subtle

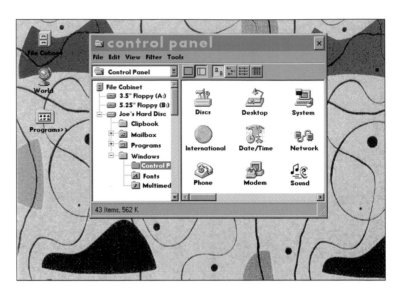

6.6 The colors and patterns used in this current desktop design were very fashionable in the designs of the 1950s.

information about both the design aesthetic and the reliability of information. Fonts say more than most people realize about content—its casualness, formality, stylishness, sophistication, and so on. [figure 6.7]

Imagery

Pictures, drawings, photographs, illustrations, maps, tables, charts, and graphs all carry strong visual messages. Imagery is one of the most powerful tools of the designer. We are always drawn to pictures before words, and we respond to them emotionally. Imagery conveys meaning both in its content and its style. We respond differently to a photograph than we do to an illustration or a chart, even though they may all contain the same data. Because of their power, images must be used very carefully so that they integrate well with and do not overpower the design. [figure 6.8]

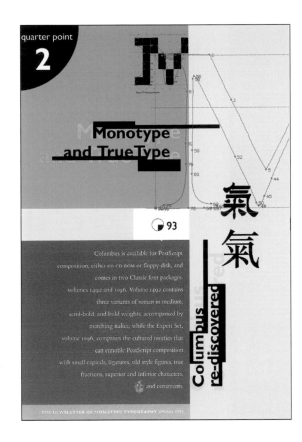

6.7 The typography on this news-letter cover from Monotype Corp-oration was designed to look stylish. The bold colors and strong layout contribute to the feeling of visual excitement, but would not be suit-able in an interface that was meant for long-term use. Photo courtesy of Monotype Typography Inc.

Graphic Design Techniques

These design techniques are essentially methods for achieving visual effects.

Arrangement

Arrangement is composition; simply, it refers to where things are put. An arrangement can create balance or imbalance, and it gives us cues about what is primary and secondary information. Reading order is an important aspect of arrangement, and this varies between cultures. In the west,

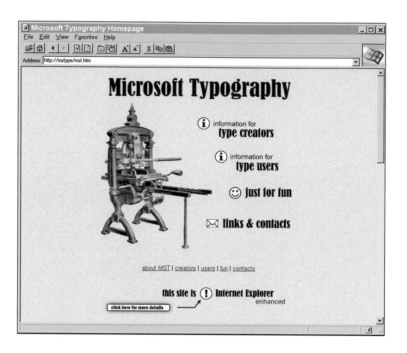

6.8 This Web home page effectively uses a large photographic image to set the tone of the website.

we read left to right and top to bottom, which influences how we compose a page or a screen. However, beautiful, balanced arrangements can be made that work in any cultural context. [figure 6.9]

Emphasis

The element that is emphasized should be the thing you see first and perceive as most important. We need emphasis to create contrast, and we use location, size, color, and font attributes such as bold, italics, or caps to create it. Emphasis is important because when all elements have equal weight, the composition is boring and hard to scan, and makes it difficult to navigate because we can't differentiate between parts. Emphasis, when employed purposefully, acts like a directional signal. Both the absence of emphasis and the wrong emphasis are common mistakes in interface design. [figure 6.10]

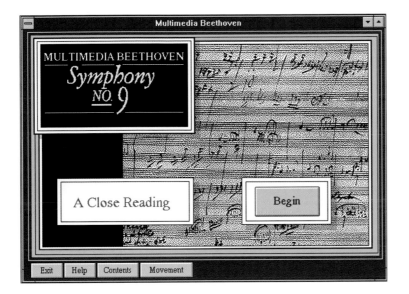

6.9 This design for Multimedia Beethoven was innovative in its time, and still works as a classic arrangement. We read the title in the upper left, then the subhead (A Close Reading), and last we see the large Begin button.

To create a pseudo-grid in dialog layouts, use precise and consistent sizes and exact alignment of controls. ❙❚

6.10 On this screen by Reuters, the dialog has the greatest emphasis, followed by the title in the upper left corner. The title serves as a focal point, drawing your attention away from the graphic and balancing the graphic, while leading you to read the instructional text below it. Designed by Rodney Edwards of interAction Graphics for Reuters, Ltd.

Focus

The focal point is usually the area of greatest emphasis, but it can be as simple as a blank space between elements that serves as a point of tension or relief. Think of the focal point as the center of attention: it's usually the spot you see first. The key is to use this technique deliberately, directing the users' focus to the area where you want them to pay attention.

Hierarchy

Visual hierarchies are very different from programming hierarchies. By hierarchy of information, designers refer to what comes first, second, and third, like levels of headings in a book. The most important overall concept (say, the chapter heading) is in the largest type size, the next in importance is somewhat smaller, and so on. Visual hierarchies communicate both the reading order and the perceived order of importance of information. [figure 6.11]

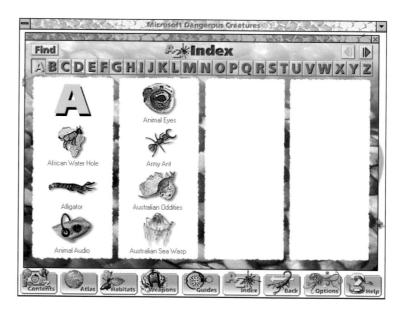

6.11 This Index screen from Microsoft Dangerous Creatures has a clear hierarchy of information presentation. The first thing you are aware of is the big letter A and the pictures of animals that start with A. Then you see the alphabet and the Index title. Because the letter A button is depressed, you can easily tell you are on the A topics in the Index. Then you notice the Find button, and last, the navigation buttons on the bottom.

Visual hierarchies are an extremely powerful organizing technique, and organized information is much easier to scan and absorb. Software interfaces often suffer from an absence of a discernible hierarchy, which leaves users roaming all over to find where to start.

Layering

Layering creates the perception of elements either in front of, behind, inside, or on top of others. It is achieved through the techniques of overlapping and containment. Layering also contributes to a sense of priority: those things behind or below are perceived as less important. Interfaces generally do a good job of layering windows on top of each other, such as using a secondary dialog as an offshoot of a main one. Sometimes, however, they do too good a job, and too many layers create confusion. Subtle visual depth cues such as drop shadows could be used more often in interface designs to help separate and distinguish multiple layers. [figure 6.12]

Grouping

Grouping creates relationships. Things in the same group are assumed to have something in common. You can use grouping to modularize or regularize a composition and create balance. You can also use grouping to convey meaning: the elements in a group should belong together. Group boxes are used successfully in Windows dialogs, but boxes aren't the only way to group items. [figure 6.13] You can create a visual group simply by placing controls next to each other, and use white space or a line to separate groups. Moreover, grouping works on a variety of levels: grouping parts of an interface into menus serves as a method for organizing it.

You can group items in a dialog just by using placement and spacing or a simple line. You don't always have to use group boxes, unless they are necessary for functional reasons. ▌▌

6.12 TaxCut tries to establish a clear hierarchy of information, but ends up with a confusing visual presentation. Where should you start: the menus, the top row of tabs, the headline text, or the selected tab in the window? To figure out what to do, you must read the text within the green tab headline, but the black on green text is very hard to see, and your attention is drawn to it last. The different tabs create different depth cues, and there is so much to look at you can't form a mental picture of where you are in the product. This is an attempt at layering that failed.

6.13 One way to avoid group boxes within group boxes is to use a line next to the group heading.

Alignment

Alignment is an extremely important, rewarding, and often overlooked technique in visual interface design. Alignment can help you achieve balance, harmony, unity, modularity, and a pleasing flow. [figure 6.14] Slight misalignments create bothersome subliminal disruptions, which are a common problem in user interface design. Consistent, exacting alignment is the easiest thing you can do to positively affect the aesthetic quality of an interface.

White Space

White space, or empty space between elements, creates breathing room. Lots of white space helps to relax the movement of the eye and makes compositions easier to parse. An absence of white space results in a feeling of complexity, and can make a design hard to read. Conversely, too much white space can become boring, but, honestly, it's hard to ever have too much white space in an interface because

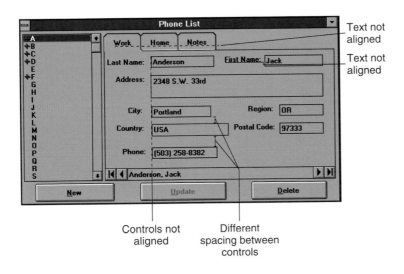

Text not aligned

Text not aligned

Controls not aligned

Different spacing between controls

6.14 Slight misalignments and uneven spacing create spatial tension, resulting in a subliminal discomfort. We focus on the edges of things, and when they don't align, we are left with a sense of clutter and disorganization, even if we don't consciously notice the misalignment.

screen real estate is always at a premium. Remember that white space is *not* unused space; it has a clear and important function: it improves readability, usability, and aesthetic quality.

One of the most common mistakes in many Windows interfaces is too narrow a left-hand margin, especially within lists. Margins are white space, too, and allow breathing room from the edges of windows or controls to the text. [figure 6.15]

Grids

True print graphic design grids are hard to achieve in user interface design, because the information often doesn't lend itself to a regular format. But interface elements heavy on

6.15 This dialog, from Microsoft Works, is an example of the haphazard results of inconsistent use of white space. The explanatory text on the right (Choose one of three…) is too close to the left edge of its inset box. This text column needs air to breathe—a space about half the size of an "n"—between the left edge of the box and the text. Conversely, there is too much space on the left side of the white listbox.

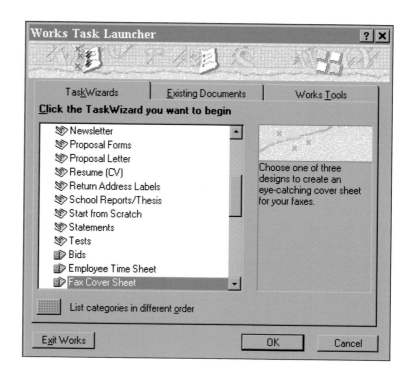

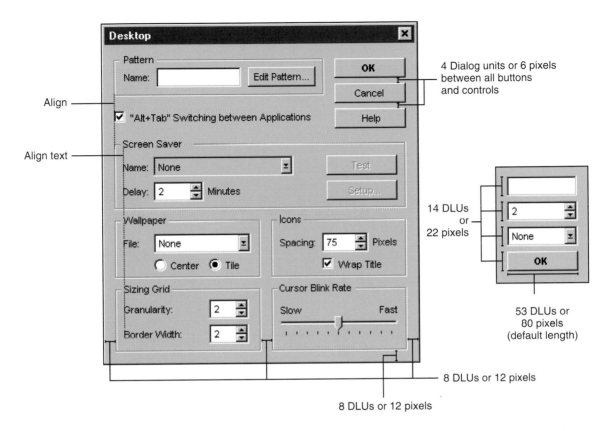

6.16 Using exact alignment to a grid will make your dialogs cleaner and more orderly. This dialog shows the Windows 95 design standards for sizes of controls and minimum spacing recommendations.

text, such as Help topics, can easily use a grid. Moreover, in windows or dialogs, you can use consistent alignments, and size the widths and heights of controls consistently. This will modularize the design, creating a modified grid that gives a sense of columns and an ordered presentation. [figure 6.16]

Part Three

Visual Perception

7

An Introduction to the Psychology of Perception

Software interfaces are often designed by argument. In the process, everyone, designers and developers alike, relates to his or her own experiences. In fact, most arguments begin with "When *I* do this, *I* . . ." because we all have the most direct knowledge of ourselves. Unfortunately, designers and developers are not typical users. Professional interface designers must get beyond their own experiences, feelings, and desires. They must instead strive to see the world through the eyes of the user—the audience. The designer must step into the users' shoes, walk around, and experience an interface the way they do.

Current Research in Perception

The accompanying quotation represents one viewpoint on the diverse but incomplete literature on perception. Current researchers use a three-part strategy, combining behavior (psychology) with computational analyses and models (neural nets), and brain biology (neural anatomy and physiology). They combine information from experiments in these three areas to build theories of how we think and perceive.

(Visual) imagery can be used in four ways: to access information stored in memory, help one reason, learn new skills, and aid comprehension of verbal descriptions.

—Stephen M. Kosslyn and Oliver Koenig, in Wet Mind, The New Cognitive Neuroscience

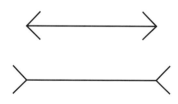

7.1 These optical illusions remind us about perceptual context. It is impossible to see both the faces and the goblet at the same time, and the arrows appear to be different lengths when they are actually the same.

Essentially, all perception is part of the process of finding meaning in the world. Earlier theorists thought perception was just an intermediate step between sensation (information received by the senses) and cognition, or thought. Current theories recognize that the backflow from thought to senses is just as strong, and see perception as a complex mediating process between thoughts and sensation. These newer theories recognize how much expectations influence perception. So the physical, psychological, and cultural context will change how we perceive something. [figure 7.1]

The Effect of the Mind on Sight

Vision is really a two-step process. Obviously, it begins with the physical characteristics of the eye, which enable us to see objects. The objects have to be large enough, with enough contrast, in a visible color, and so on, so that the eyes can register them. The physical peculiarities of human vision must therefore dictate many interface design choices, such as colors and arrangement of elements on the screen. (Details of how the human eye works will be discussed in Chapter 10.)

In the second step, retinal signals are transferred quickly to the brain, a process which requires designers to consider another level of design choices—context now becomes important. Once we can see an object clearly, we have to be able to accurately interpret what we see. In an interface, this means deciphering: Is it an icon of a folder or a small yellow blob? Is it a button that works like other buttons—something to be pressed—or does it have another meaning? [figure 7.2] This attempt to identify what we see initiates the process of building mental models.

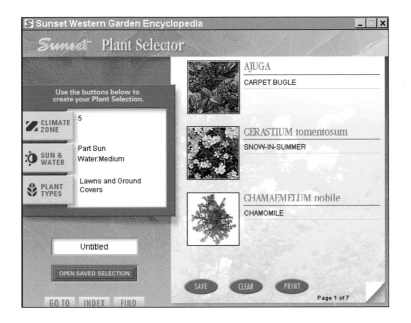

7.2 This screen from Sunset's Western Garden CD has four kinds of buttons. The designers used different buttons to group types of functions, rather than relying on other visual cues. The layout, color, and fonts help create some consistency, but the variety of buttons is somewhat disconcerting.

Mental Models

Humans are constantly constructing mental models, or paradigms, to make sense of the world. We are equipped with a tremendous amount of preprogramming that simplifies the daily navigation of our surroundings, without which we would direct most of our attention to dealing with every sensation as if it were a completely new experience. From childhood on, we build extremely complex mental models of our environment, models that are constantly being revised and updated. Interlaced with our perceptual models of the world are family and cultural viewpoints. Each culture needs to maintain a common world view to promote good communication between individuals—a common ground. Our culture and upbringing determine much of the information that we use to build mental models of the world.

Mental models or conceptual models of computer interfaces are powerful tools for good user interface design. Donald Norman is well known for his work on everyday mental models. In his popular book, *The Design of Everyday Things*, Norman describes the mental dissonances that arise from poor design, such as a door handle that looks as if it should be pushed, but really must be pulled, creating a situation where people get stopped at the door and must make multiple attempts in order to get through. Computer interfaces, too, can create cognitive dissonances when something appears to function one way, and actually works another way. [figure 7.3]

The key to forming a clear mental model is consistency: all the elements of any one type in the environment you build must be consistent with one another. For example, if you choose to show single-click pressable items as sticking up from a surface (as in Windows 95), show all single-click items in the same way. If double-clicking on one icon opens

7.3 Note the mental dissonance created by the scrollbar at the edge of the tab. It seems odd that a solid object (a 3-D tab surface meant to look like wood) should be able to move by scrolling.

the object, don't allow a single click to open another object. If you choose to construct a fantasy world for the user, such as the frog's spaceship in Explorapedia, then make sure that all the details of the spaceship are appropriate to that world; don't include a flat menu in this three-dimensional atmosphere. [figure 7.4]

People bring their own paradigms of the world and computers when they sit down in front of a keyboard and screen. This means that, in addition to building a clear and consistent conceptual model *within* the program, designers must be highly sensitive to the preconceptions that users have regarding computers. Thus, the designer must strive for internal consistency balanced with consistency with the external world. The target user's culture and background, as well his or her previous experiences with other computers and software programs must be taken into account.

It is sometimes tempting to "cheat" on consistency. But the more cohesively the parts of a presentation work together, the better the user's mental model, and therefore, the more user-friendly the interface. ▍▌

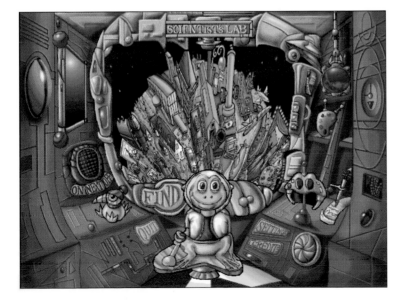

7.4 Microsoft Explorapedia creates a complete interface environment for children. It looks like fun and all the controls make sense as parts of a spaceship.

Cultural Differences

All perception is unique. Although two people may agree that a tree trunk is brown, one person can never know exactly what the second person's perception of that brown is. In Seattle's dull winter light, the tree may seem a grayish color to me, hardly brown at all. Someone else may see more of a taupe color. Still another person may just assume that since it's a tree, the trunk is medium brown. [figure 7.5]

Personal perceptions are affected by cultural influences, too. For instance, perspective is a Western phenomenon; a picture drawn in perspective is not universally perceived as three-dimensional. Using perspective as a clue for depth requires training. [figure 7.6] Historically, for example, Asian cultures depicted three dimensionality in other ways, in order to communicate the interrelated nature of experience. In much Asian art, figure and ground are equally important, like

7.5 Color perception is a very personal thing. Different people will tend to describe the colors of these trees in different ways.

7.6 During the Renaissance in Europe, mathematical relationships inspired the birth of perspective as a method of depicting depth. Perspective uses one or more vanishing points where lines converge. This painting of "The Annunciation" by Botticelli uses one-point perspective. Photo: Planet Art.

yin and yang. [figure 7.7] Western perspective techniques make the figure (the subject) appear more important than the background, which was contrary to Asian techniques, whose artists used more subtle methods, such as overlapping, to show depth. [figure 7.8]

There are many cultural differences that affect visual interface design. In user interface design, icons, and simple illustrations that would seem to leave no doubt as to their meaning in the United States might have an entirely different significance in another culture. Some icons may depict objects that don't even exist in another culture, making them unworkable. [figure 7.9] And color has many culture-specific associations. For example, in Western societies, black

7.7 The yin-yang symbol is a good example of the Asian concept of the interrelationship of foreground and background, or figure ground. In Western art, the figure is more important than the ground, but in much of Asian art, they're both important, and neither predominate.

7.8 Depth cues in Asian painting are more subtle. Overlapping creates depth, along with relative size and position: things low and larger in the picture appear closer; things smaller and higher in the picture appear farther away. Photo: Art Resource N.Y./Scala.

is worn to indicate mourning, whereas in Japan, white is worn. Some colors have religious associations, historical relevance, or other special meanings.

In addition to larger cultural differences inherent in symbols, heroes, rituals, and religion, there are always subtle language differences even when two cultures "speak the same language." For instance, what is called a trash can in the United States is a wastebasket in Great Britain and rubbish in New Zealand. Body parts, especially hands, and body gestures, also have different cultural meanings, and sometimes one culture's term can be offensive in another. Pictures of animals, people, and religious symbols also are interpreted differently among cultures. Consider cattle, which Americans think of primarily as a source of food, and which to the Indians is a sacred animal. Or think of dogs, which are pets in this country, but often are a source of food in Korea. It is remarkably easy to be offensive. [figure 7.10]

7.9 Rural route mailboxes are peculiar only to North America. Internationally, mail slots are more common. The best solution is to design a mail icon that represents the typical mail repository for your audience's region.

Individual differences combined with diverse cultural backgrounds create a vast hard-to-please audience of customers and users. We must be constantly aware that what makes sense in our world view might have a completely different effect on someone else. Beginning with that simple awareness can bring a real sophistication to design, but developing global software is just the first step. If a Windows application is going to be made available in other countries, it must be localized to those cultures. This requires not only

Localize your software with the help of native speakers. Have these "test audiences" review all icons and graphics. Then create specific alternative designs for that culture, if necessary. ▌

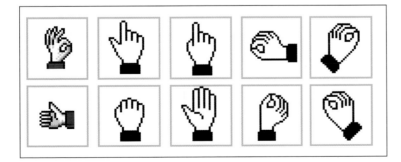

7.10 Hand gestures that are harmless in one culture may mean something offensive in another culture. Either try not to use hands in your interface, or carefully localize them for each culture.

translation of the text, but redesign of icons, images, and even dialog layouts.

Cultural Differences between Programmers and Users

In addition to broad differences among peoples, resulting from cultural peculiarities, there is another more common and pervasive difference that is peculiar in software design: that between programmers and users. Most people don't want to spend time figuring out how things work. They just want to get in their cars and drive; they don't care about engine mechanics. So it is with software. Users are task-oriented; they just want to get the job done, and they don't care how the software works. They approach their use of software as a process: step 1, step 2, step 3, and so on, without paying attention to the underlying structure. [figure 7.11]

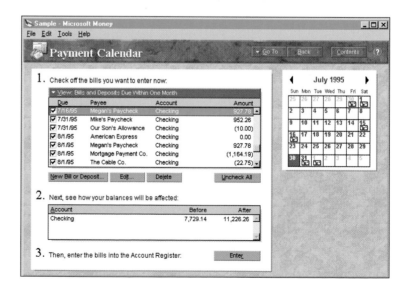

7.11 Microsoft Money 4.0 is a good example of a successful task-based interface.

Engineers, on the other hand, love to figure out how things work. They really enjoy constructing mental models of their world. A great engineer is someone who is good at solving mental puzzles, building structures that fit together, and creating something that functions well.

This "cultural difference," which really is an experiential difference, has resulted in a common problem in Windows interface designs: needless complexity. An engineer may see an opportunity to enable a minor function, and it is easy for the engineer to figure out both how to implement it and then how to use it because the underlying structure is obvious to him or her. But to the user, this minor function may add complexity, getting in the way of performing the major task. The user doesn't see its relationship to the structure, and finds it confusing.

The Psychological Environment of Windows

People take their cues from their environments, and they have different expectations based on their life experiences. This is another reason for aiming for consistent integration of systems software and other Windows programs. Users have experience with other programs and have developed methods for using them. The Windows environment sets up certain psychological expectations, and if something works one way in the system, users expect it to work the same way in application software.

8

Affordances, Realism, and Dimension

"Affordance" is a popular interface design concept taken from the world of psychology. It means a subtle design characteristic that conveys the correct use of an object. Many affordances in our everyday lives are subtle and often go unnoticed, such as the downward curved shape of a door handle, the placement of knobs on a stove, or the height of a button that slightly rises up from the surface beneath it. The design of the door handle naturally directs us to push down, the knobs relate to the layout of the burner, the button invites pressing. [figure 8.1]

Why Are Affordances Important to Visual Interface Design?

Affordances make interfaces intuitive, because we instinctively understand them. We carry over paradigms from our "real" physical world to the software interface. They help us guess functions correctly because of their size, shape, and relationship to other elements on the screen.

Affordances take advantage of perception. A small shadow behind one window makes it stand out from other windows, making it seem more active. A few pixels of highlight and shadow can create an easily seen button. A

8.1 This door handle was designed to afford pushing down; the buttons above were designed to afford pressing.

slider that mimics one found on a stereo system makes its horizontal motion more obvious. [figure 8.2]

Let's apply these concepts to a real-world problem. For instance, turning pages, rather than scrolling them, is an obvious real-world action. But how can we design a control with affordances for page turning? Well, we can start with a turned-over corner, but let's not forget the subtleties. Should the corner be on the top of the page or the bottom? How big should we make the dog-ear? How can we convey that the corner is activated by clicking once? For starters, a shadow

8.2 This slider from the Display Properties dialog from Windows 95 makes its function clear by its resemblance to sliders in the real world.

can make this image more action-oriented. [figure 8.3]
Another way we can communicate page turning is to use two
buttons with arrows and the page number between. [figure 8.4]

Affordances also connect parts of an interface. Once an
affordance helps a user discover a function instinctively, it sets
up a mental model for other similar affordances to make sense.
A paradigm is constructed without the user being aware of it.

Three-Dimensional in a Two-Dimensional Space

How much dimensionality is necessary in a Windows
application? Again, it depends on the context.

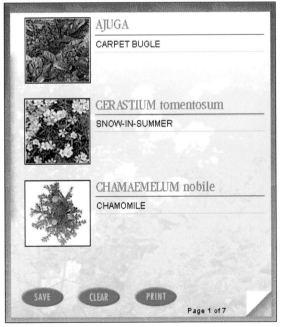 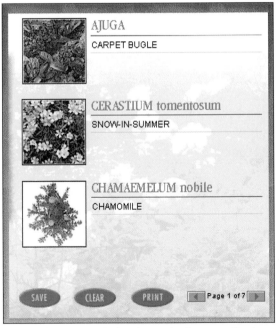

8.3 The dog-eared corner of this document is an
affordance for page flipping because of its similarity to
the real world.

8.4 In this alternate design, the paging buttons afford
single-click pressing, but the overall metaphor is more
abstract.

Realism vs. Abstraction

Windows 95 is a two-dimensional presentation of a shallow, three-dimensional world. Realistic icons, pictures, spaces, and three-dimensional controls help with recognition. In fact, most successful consumer CD titles use a high degree of realism, because it enables users to understand and enjoy the products more. [figure 8.5] The Windows operating system uses semirealistic 3-D controls because they are more intuitive. [figure 8.6] But realism also wastes space. Compared to the dense abstraction of a map, a software interface communicates much less information, and is much harder to scan and decipher.

Human perception is fundamentally three-dimensional. We are used to seeing, locating, and working with objects in space. Flat, abstracted graphics can be very effective when the paradigm is fairly universal, as in maps. [figure 8.7] But maps don't make sense to everyone. Mapping a bird's-eye view of

8.5 In a children's CD title, a spaceship control room metaphor is a perfectly viable design option.

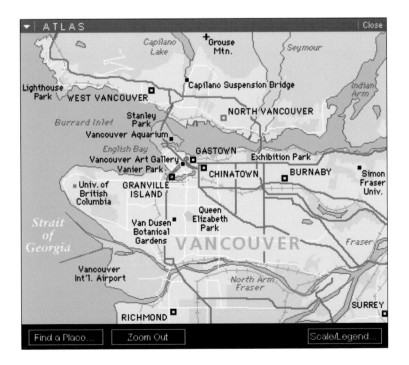

8.6 The subtle 3-D effects in Windows 95 create a great degree of affordance for the user.

8.7 This map of Vancouver, British Columbia, from Microsoft Encarta will help some people find the Van Dusen Botanical Gardens, but others will prefer a verbal description of which roads to take.

the three-dimensional world is a difficult task, impossible for some people. If, for example, you give directions to your house, some people will prefer a map, and others will prefer a verbal description.

Some products take three-dimensionality and realism to an even higher degree, creating fake spaces such as rooms, buildings, and streets. Products like Magic Cap, Microsoft Bob, and For Your Eyes Only make great use of metaphors to make the user comfortable, but pay the price in terms of the density of information that can be displayed on the screen. [figures 8.8 and 8.9]

Rat's-Eye View vs. Bird's-Eye View

Mark Malamud and Edward Jung, interface researchers at Microsoft, call the difference between realism and abstraction a rat's-eye view and a bird's-eye view. A rat's-eye view is

8.8 For Your Eyes Only, an art history title for children, uses engaging, realistic objects as nonverbal interface controls. These controls remain on the edges of the screen, and animate as children move the mouse over them.

8.9 Computer-generated 3-D environments are popular because they are a magical distorted version of the real world. But very little detailed information can be shown in this kind of interface.

realistic because you're down in the maze and experience the world from inside it. You feel the walls to figure out where you are, and see things directly. This view is tactile and familiar. Users of the early Macintosh had this experience because they opened up folders and saw documents "within" them. In contrast, a bird's-eye view is abstract, like a map. You have the advantage of seeing the whole world, but without the experiential quality possible from within. DOS and early Windows offered a bird's-eye view, using elaborate tree structures to show you where you were. Because abstraction is often hard to grasp, the bird's-eye view has limitations, but it can provide incredible density and power. Malamud and Jung believe that an important part of creating a new interface is determining, at the beginning, whether you are developing a rat's-eye or a bird's-eye view, and then being consistent to that perspective.

Three-Dimensionality Is a Powerful Affordance

Currently, Windows is the most common interface on personal computers. Although the windows-on-a-desktop metaphor has some drawbacks, it works well enough that it is widely accepted. When it is combined with a 3-D presentation style, as in Windows 95, it becomes more "rat's-eye" and hence less abstract.

Three-dimensional controls in the Windows interface, when they are depicted both subtly and systematically, result in a consistent paradigm. Once users have learned that items that are raised can be pressed, items that are recessed cannot, and items on a flat white background can be opened, edited, or moved, they carry that knowledge over to new situations with new programs. They expect work areas to be white and unobstructed. They expect controls that appear higher than the window surface to respond when pressed. Users only have to look and react, they don't need to remember which words or colored areas perform which functions. A consistent, subtle 3-D environment is familiar and predictable, and takes less time to learn. [figure 8.10]

Advantages of Flat Interfaces

The major drawbacks to 3-D interfaces are that the 3-D details take up extra space, and can easily get complex when overused. Flat graphical presentations take longer to learn, but they are visually simpler. Given a small screen with a lot of information to present, every pixel of simplification is helpful. Windows 95 chose usability over graphic simplicity and incorporates a consistent set of 3-D controls; they are simple and subtle, while remaining visible.

Some interfaces, such as Encarta 95, use flat graphics in combination with animation and sound to convey function.

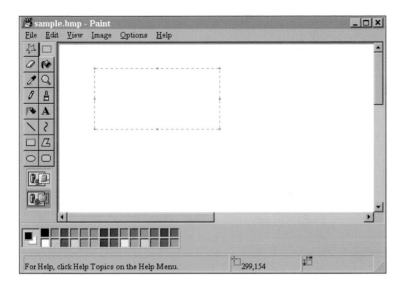

8.10 The Windows 95 Paint interface is clean, simple, and easy to figure out.

The flat, colored title areas are much cleaner visually than if they were 3-D bars. And by giving feedback when the mouse moves over them, they indicate that they are clickable. [figure 8.11]

Common 3-D Pitfalls

The most common error made with using three-dimensionality is the same one people make when they cook: if a little spice is good, then more will be better. But 3-D effects work well on a computer screen only when they are subtle. Too much 3-D is ugly, distracting, and confusing, especially in the constricted pseudo-reality of software environments. [figure 8.12]

The other common mistake is to use an inconsistent 3-D representation. Software designers and developers often overlook the fine details of their 3-D controls, which is risky, because it's those subtle details that create affordances and a

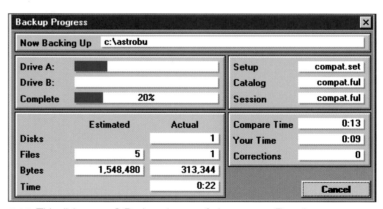

8.11 Although Encarta uses a flat interface, it is still easy to determine which areas of the screen are active, because they move when the mouse passes over them.

8.12 This dialog uses 3-D plates in a confusing manner. First, they are inconsistent with the rest of the system, so the user has no prior knowledge of their meaning. Second, they divide the information into sections that look meaningful, but actually are not. For instance, the white bars with drop shadows show both progress bars and text. The text appears editable, but it is not. Moreover, the most important item in the dialog, the percentage indicating that the entire backup is complete—Complete 20%—is buried between other controls and looks equivalent in importance to Drive A: and Drive B:.

clear paradigm. Sometimes, for example, the highlight and shadow details are inconsistent within the application itself. More often, there are inconsistencies between the application and the operating system. [figure 8.13]

3-D in Windows 3.1 and Windows 95

Windows 95 has a consistent 3-D appearance, unlike the combination of flat and 3-D in Windows 3.1. It uses an upper left-hand light source and eliminates the black lines that completely surround controls in Windows 3.1. The 3-D system of borders and fills was designed so that all controls fit and work together in a modular fashion. [figure 8.14]

If you are developing a business application that will be used within the Windows desktop environment, use the 3-D paradigm of the operating system. Be consistent, use the controls provided; don't Invent new controls or new interactions. Read and follow the Windows 95 interface style guide. If you have to create a new control, use the Border Styles API, so that the details of your 3-D match the operating system. ▌▌

8.13 The tools in this toolbox are both hard to see and confusing, because of their strange 3-D presentation. The tool graphics are cut in oddly to the button surface, and the selected tool has a tentative gray raised graphic. These pseudo-3-D effects are inconsistent and unclear.

8.14 The details of the 3-D borders in Windows 95 were designed to fit together. Note in the toolbar buttons how the edges of the up button and the pressed button fit cleanly next to each other.

8.15 Microsoft Explorapedia, The World of Nature, uses a globe and ecology metaphor for navigation to topics.

When developing a consumer application, consistency with the operating system might hamper the impact of your content. In this situation you will have to create a new complete paradigm within your application. As with a game application, you will need to create an environment, rules, and affordances of your own. Use realism, animation, sound, cursor feedback, and other cues to make your interface intuitive. [figure 8.15] Use the operating system controls and paradigm when it applies to the content.

9

Design for the Screen

Designing for the computer screen poses unique problems and provides unique opportunities. As in any design practice, it's important to know the characteristics of the medium so that you can solve problems and take advantage of opportunities. On-screen images are produced at very low resolution compared with images printed on paper. Even the most sophisticated interface is harder to read than magazines, books, or newspapers. Interfaces have less real information (less text, data, and pictures), and many functional graphic elements that are necessary for navigation, such as scrollbars, toolbars, title bars, miscellaneous buttons, icons, and character agents. The controls and window elements add to the complexity of the screen, and take space and attention away from the central content, the document.

Tests have shown that people read screen text more slowly than text on paper. So, in addition to losing space to controls and window elements, text is more difficult to read. Both of these factors put computer screens at a disadvantage when competing with the visual sophistication of printed materials. [figure 9.1]

```
┌─────────────────────────────────────────────────────────┐
│ ⊞ Windows Help                              _ □ ✕        │
├─────────────────────────────────────────────────────────┤
│ Help Topics │   Back   │   Options   │                   │
├─────────────────────────────────────────────────────────┤
│ To add a new submenu to the Programs menu               │
│ 1 Use the right mouse button to click the Start button, │
│   and then click Open.                                  │
│ 2 Double-click the Programs folder.                     │
│ 3 Click the File menu, and then point to New.           │
│ 4 Click Folder, and then type the name that you want to │
│   use for the submenu.                                  │
│ 5 Press ENTER, and then double-click the folder you     │
│   just created.                                         │
│ 6 On the File menu, point to New, and then click        │
│   Shortcut.                                             │
│ 7 Use the Create Shortcut wizard to add items to the    │
│   submenu.                                              │
│ ─────────────────────────────────────────────────       │
│ ▪ Related Topics                                        │
└─────────────────────────────────────────────────────────┘
```

9.1 This help topic is one example of the appearance of text on the screen. There is less text, less color and graphics, and less information than in the printed equivalent.

Function vs. Decoration

Although visual interface design *looks* like graphic design—two-dimensional elements communicate information—interface design *works* like industrial design—functions are revealed by three-dimensional forms. Like industrial products, every pixel in an interface has a perceived function or purpose, so designers can't use traditional graphic decoration, because it creates confusion. When one symbol indicates an action, but another symbol is purely decorative, users will be confused. This goes back to the issue of consistency—types of elements should have similar functions. [figure 9.2]

Decoration used ineffectively can be confusing and distract the user from finding real information. Every pixel should have a function—but this does not mean that pictures or illustrations can't or shouldn't be used. In fact, a simple

9.2 Microsoft Works 3.0 uses a confusing illustration. The gray drop-shadowed boxes look as though they might be clickable interface elements, but they have no function other than to fill up the right side of the screen.

illustration, like the key on a map, can greatly enhance the interactivity of a program feature. The function of the picture is to illustrate, and users will understand that, as long as the illustration is presented clearly. [figure 9.3]

On-Screen Perceptual Issues

As mentioned, design for the screen raises several visual perception issues unique to software.

Screen Resolution

Many types of computer monitors are available in the market, which causes headaches for both designers and developers, because they must create software that can both run and look good on a wide variety of devices, and in many colors and resolutions. The physical size of the monitor is as much a factor as the pixel resolution and the available colors. For

One method for dealing with screen differences is to pick one size and color set, and optimize for that, making sure that your product runs (but accepting that it may not look as good) on other resolutions. It is even better, however, to design a variety of sizes and colors, and allow the user to choose between them—for example, the wide variety of control panel settings for Windows 95. ∎

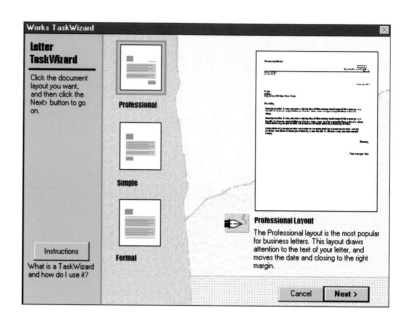

9.3 Works for Windows 95 uses thumbnail graphics in its wizards, with subtle textures as background organizing elements. This is a good example of meaningful illustration in an interface, because the thumbnail pictures have a clear function.

instance, the size of a pixel on a 19" monitor at 1024×768 resolution is much bigger than the size of a pixel on a 15" monitor with the same resolution. Of course, larger pixels are easier to see.

Unfortunately, there is no perfect solution for this dilemma. The best you can do is to design for the most common screen resolution and number of colors that your target market uses. Market research is the only reliable method for getting this information. Many developers use their best guess, for instance, if a user has a CD drive, he or she is likely to have a newer, higher resolution monitor.

For Windows 95, the target monitor is 800×600, 256 colors. But be sure to also test and refine your design in other resolutions and colors. Many users still have VGA 16-color screens, and VGA resolution (640×480) is common on laptop computers. There are also many users who have

1024 × 768-resolution monitors and millions of colors
(24-bit color). Consequently, you must not only look at your
designs in these other screen configurations, but you should
also design alternatives for them as well.

Designing for the television screen can be even more
difficult, due to interlacing, which refers to the alternating
horizontal lines of phosphor dots used to create TV images;
it can cause various visual distortions in text and lines.
Although interlacing works fine for realistic moving images,
it can make lines or shapes vibrate, change color, or even
disappear. Another problem is artifacting, which is the color
distortion that occurs when certain colors are placed next to
each other, created by the triangular arrangement of red,
green, and blue phosphor in the tube (similar, but more
subtle, effects occur on computer monitors, as well).

Windows developers need to worry about these effects
only when they work on interactive TV applications or
design software for computer/TV hybrids. In fact, designing
for a television screen is so different from designing for a
typical computer screen that the details are beyond the scope
of this book.

Jaggies

Low-resolution pixels on a computer screen are big and
chunky, and their appearance is often referred to as jaggies or
stairsteps, because they have no smooth angles or curves.
Obviously, the jagged edges make text harder to read and
pictures unclear. [figure 9.4]

Antialiasing, the process of adding gray pixels to jagged
edges, can help smooth lines. But, antialiasing must be used
carefully, because it also makes lines fuzzier, less sharp. [figure

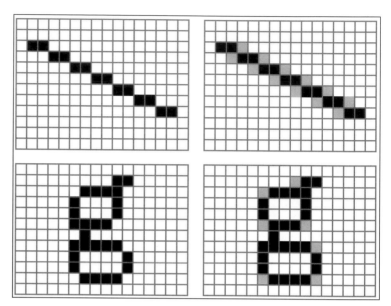

9.4 Jagged pixels on a computer screen make any image that is angled or curved harder to see. Antialiasing, also called grayscaling, uses gray or colored pixels to smooth angles and curves.

9.5] Further, antialiasing does not work well for small text, nor on the outside edges of icons or elements where the background color can change. [figure 9.6] It is best used on the interior of illustrations and icons, and with larger fonts, ideally shown in black on a white background. [figure 9.7]

The Lightbox Effect

Many studies have evaluated the perceptual effects of reading. They indicate that contrast has a strong effect on reading speed and comprehension: when the light/dark contrast between the text and the background is insufficient, reading slows considerably; conversely, a very bright white background can be too shocking to the eyes and also create

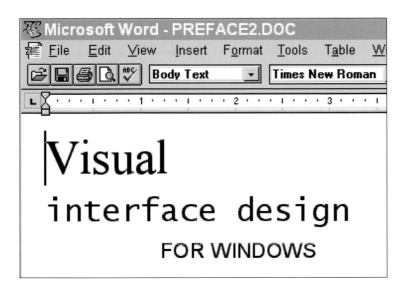

9.5 High-quality automatic antialiasing of fonts is available in the Windows 95 Plus Pack, but it must be done by hand for graphics or icons.

reading difficulty. Notice, for example, how many books are printed on off-white or buff-colored paper, in order to achieve the optimum contrast level. Even greater problems occur when the background paper color is too dark behind black text, resulting in too little contrast.

The effects are somewhat different on a computer screen than on paper, however. Looking at a computer monitor is like looking into a light bulb—the brightness of computer white is very high. This can cause eye fatigue, and it is fundamentally different from looking at light reflected off paper. Even so, good contrast is still important for readability. Complicating the dilemma is that the amount of relative contrast needed for optimum readability varies widely between individuals. Therefore, it is important that users be able to change both text and background colors to obtain the best contrast for their eyes. [figure 9.8]

9.6 Antialiasing the edges of icons with gray pixels doesn't work on all backgrounds. For icons, use the Windows interface style guide recommendations.

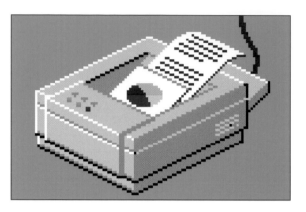

9.7 Antialiasing lines within an illustration can dramatically improve the quality of the illustration.

Color Problems

On systems where the color depth is less than 8 bits per pixel (less than 256 colors), screen colors are both limited and too bright for either good design or readability. With only a few bright colors to pick from, it is difficult to employ the many subtle strategies necessary for good graphic design. [figure 9.9] Until 16- or 24-bit color is universal, visual interface designers have to be very careful with color, and often must develop workarounds. Windows 95 uses an internal standard

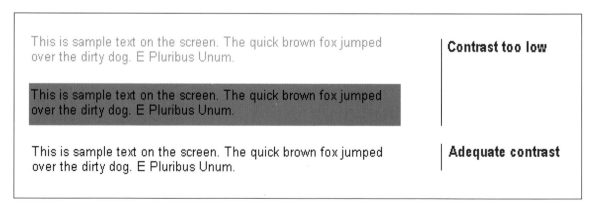

This is sample text on the screen. The quick brown fox jumped over the dirty dog. E Pluribus Unum.

Contrast too low

This is sample text on the screen. The quick brown fox jumped over the dirty dog. E Pluribus Unum.

This is sample text on the screen. The quick brown fox jumped over the dirty dog. E Pluribus Unum.

Adequate contrast

9.8 Good contrast is essential for legibility of on-screen text.

256-color palette, which applications can also load. This minimizes flashing and strange color changes when users switch between applications. [figure 9.10]

Screen Real Estate

Real estate on the screen is always at a premium. The screen is too small and too low resolution to successfully display the quantity of complex information in everyday software programs. This conflict is unresolvable: we have many complex ideas and functions to present, and never enough

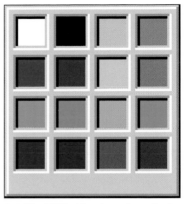

9.9 The VGA 16-color palette limits good design. Softer, subtler colors are usually more effective.

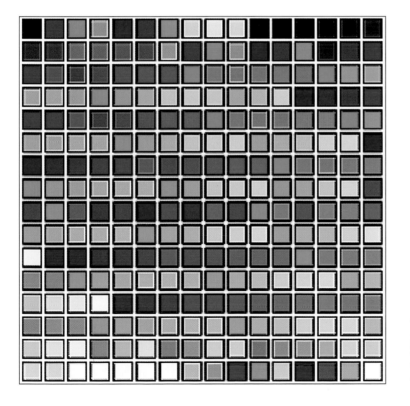

9.10 When possible, use this palette, the Windows 95 standard 256-color palette. Or, design your own 256-color palette and load it with your application.

9.11 This Windows 3.1 design for BP Service View is an example of good refinement of a variety of elements presented in a very small space. Although there are too many borders, they are minimized with the use of gray backgrounds in two shades. Color is used as a focal point to indicate the view chosen (the Service button has a yellow line, which draws your eye to it), and to draw attention to the tool button on the left side. Design by Ron Bird of interAction graphics, Ltd., UK.

space to do so adequately. The only solution is economy of presentation. As described in Chapter 5 on graphic design, refining, reducing, and simplifying are the best methods for achieving this goal. [figure 9.11]

The Expense of Graphics

Using graphics in screen design raises a practical issue. Because beautiful, highly detailed graphic images are large files that take up a lot of memory and disk space, they can be slow to load, they can slow down the primary software functions, and they can take up so much disk space that it often isn't feasible to include them. Designers and programmers have invented many workarounds for this problem. Compression is the best solution, and object-oriented graphics are much easier to compress than bitmapped graphics. Unfortunately, it's harder to draw great-looking pictures as object-oriented graphics (with draw programs such as Illustrator, Freehand, or Corel Draw).

Highly rendered photographic style bitmaps are more beautiful, and usually easier to recognize, but take up more space and are harder to compress. [figure 9.12]

Designers usually try to strike a compromise between these extremes for most interface graphics. Some techniques include using smaller bitmaps, using fewer of them, and using line drawings where possible. Publishing on a CD gives you more disk space, but you must also contend with the slow speed of the CD drive.

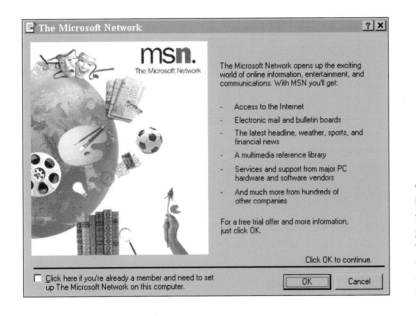

9.12 The start-up bitmap for the Microsoft Network sets the tone for the content to follow. Start-up graphics are often bitmaps, because they appear every time the application opens and work like advertising materials to convey an emotional sense of the product.

Part Four

Visual Design Elements

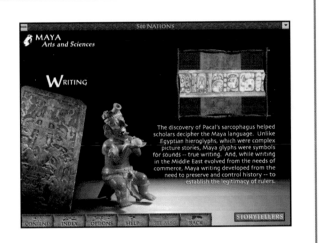

10

Color

Of all the visual elements of screen design, color is the most
controversial. Everyone loves color, and we are attracted to
colors instinctively—the result of thousands of years of
human evolution. And everyone has opinions about color. It
plays a major role in fashion and style: of clothes, furniture,
cars, and the myriad objects in our lives. It is important in art
forms all over the world, both indigenous and modern. [figure
10.1] Color is enjoyed, debated, and used by humans for many
purposes, and there are as many definitions of a pleasing
color as there are people in the world.

10.1 Bright colors are a hallmark
of the art of Mexico and many
indigenous art forms throughout
the world. Photo: Leo de Wys
Inc./Steve Vidler.

The Eye

In school, most of us learned something about the structure of the human eye. [figure 10.2] To refresh your memory, we have two kinds of light receptors in our eyes: rods and cones. Rods register light and dark, or the relative brightness of objects. There are many more rods in the eye than cones, and they respond slowly to changes in levels of light. However, once adjusted, it is the rods that enable our night vision. Cones perceive color, and there are three kinds of cones in the eye, those that respond primarily to red light, those that respond primarily to green light, and those that respond primarily to blue. There are about the same number of red and green cones, but fewer blue cones. And there are very few blue cones in the fovea, the focusing center of the eye. The information from these rods and cones is transferred to the optic nerve and sent to the brain, which is where we actually perceive color.

10.2 This diagram of the structure of the eye, from Microsoft Encarta, shows both the fovea, the focusing center of the eye, and the blind spot, where the optic nerve attaches to the retina.

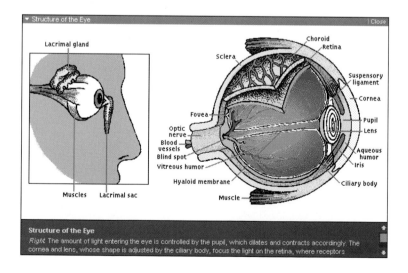

Color Systems

We are such a visually dependent species that artists and scientists have been trying to decipher our visual perceptions for a long time. Several color systems have been developed to document the millions of different colors that we can discriminate. Physics uses mathematical formulas to describe the visible colors in wavelengths of light. Artists use color wheels with primary and secondary colors. For most color systems, three qualities are important.

Any color can be broken down into red, green, and blue wavelengths—which matches the cones in our eyes. The three wavelengths multiply to yield the wavelength of the individual color. Colors used on computer monitors and TV screens are described in terms of RGB—red, green, blue. [figure 10.3] We can also divide a color into hue, saturation, and value (HSV). Hue is the color name, such as red, orange, or yellow. Saturation is the relative intensity of the color, from brilliant to dull. Value is the relative lightness or darkness of the color. These three qualities can also be quantified mathematically and combined to describe any color, just like RGB.

Printed or painted colors, which are seen as light reflected from a surface, can also be described in terms of hue, saturation, and value. However, instead of using HSV values, printers usually mix a solid color of ink (often using the Pantone system), or create a photographic color by combining tiny dots of color in a process called a halftone. These small dots are printed in varying amounts of CMYK, or cyan, magenta, yellow, and black.

Different color systems are used in science, technology, art, and business. The Munsell system has been used primarily by artists. The CIE systems, which were developed

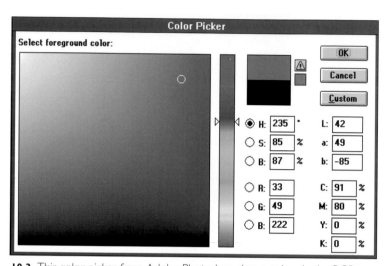

10.3 This color picker from Adobe Photoshop shows colors in the RGB (red, green, blue) color space. It includes a button with a caution symbol that appears when the color chosen cannot be printed, because the gamut of colors available on a monitor is not the same as the colors available in inks or dyes. It also indicates color values as numbers in four different color spaces: hue saturation and brightness (HSB or HSV); the screen colors of red, green, blue (RGB); the physics/math color space of CIE Lab; and the printer's primaries of cyan, magenta, yellow and black (CMYK).

by the Commission Internationale d'Eclairage in the 1920s, have been updated several times, and are in common use by scientists and color-imaging software. [figure 10.4] HSV, CMYK, and the Pantone system are used by graphic professionals and artists. (If you are interested in knowing more about color science, refer to the many excellent resources listed at the end of this book.)

Perceptual Effects of Color: A Summary of Findings

In addition to experiments on the anatomy of the eye and the physics of light, scientists have also conducted studies of the

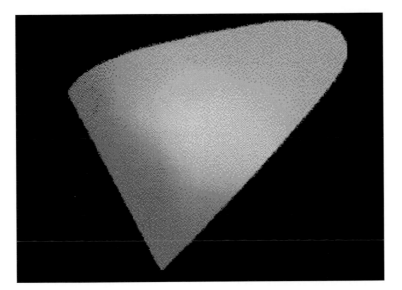

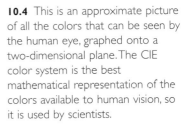

10.4 This is an approximate picture of all the colors that can be seen by the human eye, graphed onto a two-dimensional plane. The CIE color system is the best mathematical representation of the colors available to human vision, so it is used by scientists.

psychological effects of color. The color information received in the eye is transferred to the brain, where there is a great deal of variability of response between individuals. There is much conflicting information about color perception, and many results don't apply to color on the screen as they do to printed colors. Nevertheless, a few widely accepted perceptual effects of color are commonly agreed upon by researchers.

Color Is Emotional

Color has emotional properties: red excites the eye and blue calms it. People ascribe feelings to colors: she was so angry she saw red, he was green with envy, he is yellow (he is a coward). We instinctively evaluate the state of the world around us based on color cues: fire is red and casts an orange glow; a healthy person has a rosy blush on his or her cheeks; a sick person looks pale and yellow. Fresh meat is a bright red, old meat is brown; many fresh vegetables are deep green, but turn yellow or brown when they are past their prime. We see beauty in a teal green sea, a yellow flower, or the blue of a loved-one's eyes. [figure 10.5]

There is both a physical and a psychological basis for the emotional qualities of color. Some wavelengths of light (such as red) excite the neurons in the brain more than others. But our delight in a field of wildflowers or our sense of isolation in an endlessly brown desert are probably survival adaptations. The level of emotional response to color, and the fact that it varies considerably from person to person, has important implications for the design of visual interfaces. Each of us has colors that we love and colors that we hate. I am not fond of pink; one good friend hates yellow, while another is crazy about yellow and thinks it's the best color on the planet; few people dislike blue. When it comes to all the colors we can perceive, everyone has strong feelings. [figure 10.6]

Be careful with color! Always let the user choose the color. If you hard code a color that you like, someone else is sure to hate it. The more colors that users can set for themselves, the happier they will be. And, if you have many color settings, give users some help by providing a variety of color schemes that are designed to work well together and that appeal to a wide variety of tastes. ▮▮

10.5 This quiet landscape appears peaceful because of our emotional associations with the familiar colors in it. Photo: Leo de Wys, Inc./Fridmar Damm.

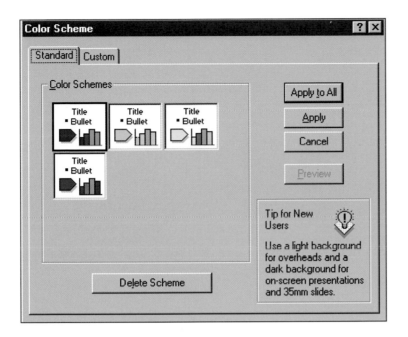

10.6 One way to deal with the wide variation in emotional reaction to color is to give users several color schemes to choose from. Microsoft Powerpoint, and other products where graphics are important, have done this for a long time. But all software products should allow customizable color schemes.

Color Has Cultural Associations

We associate red with danger: stop lights and stop signs are red, so are fire extinguishers. We associate yellow with caution: yellow lights, yield signs, barricades. Green stands for go, okay, turn on, and, in the United States, for money. Purple is a regal color in European cultures, whereas in Asia, emperors wear red. A few colors have achieved cross-cultural associations, because of the modern globalization of culture. Red and green are used for stop and go almost everywhere in the world. [figure 10.7] But there are some very specific cultural associations that don't cross culturize. As noted in a previous chapter, black is worn to indicate mourning in many Western societies, whereas white is worn in Japan. Color associations also relate to the rituals and arts of a culture. In the West we think of the red and green combination as Christmas colors. [figure 10.8] Most religions

10.7 The color red is good for drawing attention, which is why it is used for stop signs and fire extinguishers.

10.8 The colors red and green have a cultural association for Christians with the Christmas holidays. Photo: Planet Art.

and societies similarly identify certain colors with festivals, holidays, and traditions.

Colors Draw Attention

In a black-and-white field, we will instantly see a colored object. In a field of colors, we will see the brightest (most saturated) color first. Color attracts the eye, and once the eye is engaged, attention quickly focuses on the object. [figure 10.9]

The attention-getting quality of bright colors explains why important signage and objects for children are brightly colored. Stop signs are bright red so that we notice them quickly. Circuses are full of bright colors to excite the eye; they communicate the feeling of frenzied activity. [figure 10.10]

Bright colors are exciting and attract more attention, but they also can be more distracting than softer or less intense colors. The best color combinations for productivity software are usually soft, quiet, and less brilliant. Too many bright colors may make an interface seem disorganized and frenetic. ▌▌

10.9 In a computer game, brightly colored text and numbers are used to stand out against a neutral background.

Colors Relate or Group Elements

Did you ever think about why people prefer to have clothes in matching colors? Researchers agree that we often use color for grouping or relating things to each other. A shirt and pants of the same color become an outfit, and, to some, there

10.10 The tabs in Lotus 1-2-3 grab visual attention away from the menus, toolbar buttons, and the text headline. All these colors make it hard to decide where to look first, and since the tabs are different colors, it's hard to tell which tab is selected.

is something satisfying about towels that match the shower curtain. In a field of abstract shapes, many will assume that all the red objects are related in some way, all the blue objects in another way, and so on. [figure 10.11]

In an office setting, color is often used to group information. I place all my research articles in blue folders, my correspondence in yellow folders, and my finances in green folders to help me locate information. Similarly, in a dentist's office, file folders of all patients whose names begin with A may be marked in one color, with B in another color, and so on. Thanks to this color grouping, a misfiled folder stands out readily.

Color Coding Is Not Always Fast

Color coding works when we mentally group objects by color. However, we are slow to associate a color with an abstract concept. We see the color, and then have to translate that color in the brain to a specific meaning, which takes mental processing time. Color codes are most effective

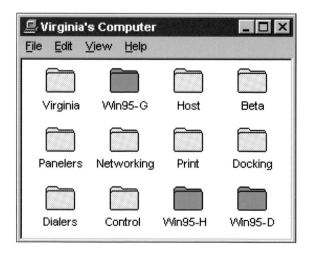

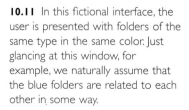

10.11 In this fictional interface, the user is presented with folders of the same type in the same color. Just glancing at this window, for example, we naturally assume that the blue folders are related to each other in some way.

when there aren't too many of them, they are used repetitively, and are associated with a common cultural use of color. Again, the best example is red because we associate it with danger. Color codes also work well when they have some personal reference. I am somewhat faster to associate a meaning with a color when I have determined the association myself. It takes me longer to learn color codes that have been predetermined by others. [figure 10.12]

Colors Influence Other Colors

In a photograph of a bunch of flowers, we may initially perceive one as white, but when a single petal is isolated, we see that it is actually pink. But seen as a whole, the brain combines all the color cues in the flower and interprets the color as white. [figure 10.13] Sometimes one color next to another can cause a complete color misinterpretation—what was yellow appears orange, for instance, depending on the color surrounding it. [figure 10.14]

Some colors placed next to each other in certain configurations can't be focused on at the same time (such as red and green) and create a vibrating effect—the colors seem to move, which can be very disturbing. [figure 10.15] Colors that are very similar in both hue and value will also cause visual discomfort when seen next to each other, because the eye has to strain to distinguish the slight difference. [figure 10.16]

Blue Is Hard to Focus

It is difficult to focus the color blue for three reasons: there are few blue cones in the human eye, very few in the fovea, and the wavelength of blue light actually focuses in front of

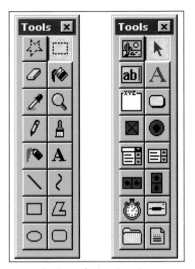

10.12 In these fictional tool palettes, the colors of the icons convey different meanings. When the colors are simply used to illustrate an object, they help us recognize the icon. However, when color is used arbitrarily, we assume the colors have special meaning, when in fact they don't.

In a Windows interface, use colors to group or relate information and to attract attention where you want it. Don't use colors arbitrarily; users assume that colors are important or related in some way. Only use color coding for a small number of items that will be used all the time, and try to associate colors with common meanings, such as danger and caution. ▮▮

10.13 We assume all the petunias are white, even though some petals in the photograph are actually a lavender color, because they are in shadow.

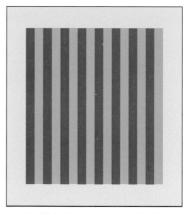

10.14 Colors look different depending on the colors next to them. The central square in these four graphics is the exact same shade of red, but it appears brighter or lighter or darker, depending on the color next to it.

10.15 Note how these vertical bars of red and green create a vibrating effect.

the fovea. This human physiological peculiarity means that blue is a great background color, but it does not work well in small areas, thin fonts, or narrow lines. [figure 10.17]

Color Deficiencies and Color Blindness

True red-green color blindness is rare, affecting less than 1 percent of the human population. However, about 9 percent of males have some form of color deficiency or color confusion, whereas color deficiencies in women are very rare. These deficiencies vary considerably; for instance, some men have trouble distinguishing a hue when the values of a set of colors are dark and closely related, hence the standard joke about being unable to distinguish dark green from navy or dark brown socks. Other men have trouble with hue differences when the colors are light in value.

Don't use blue for small areas or thin lines, and be careful about which colors you place next to each other. Take into account human color deficiencies, and never use color as the sole means of conveying information; always use color as a redundant cue. ▌▌

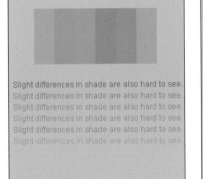

10.16 These slight differences in shades of green are difficult to perceive, especially in text.

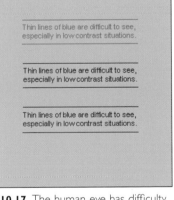

10.17 The human eye has difficulty focusing small areas of blue as a foreground color, but it works well as a background color.

As noted earlier in the book, because the perception of color is an internal one, we can never know exactly how someone else sees a color. Careful use of color can enhance the feeling of realism and the perceived friendliness of an interface. But haphazard use of color can cause real problems and communicate unintended feelings.

11

Icons and Imagery

Icons have been used in graphical user interfaces since the design of the first graphical interface, the Xerox Star. Icons have persisted for two practical reasons: people are instinctively drawn to pictures, and icons prove to be an ideal shorthand. In the limited space of a computer monitor, one small icon can stand for a large, complex object or program. [figure 11.1]

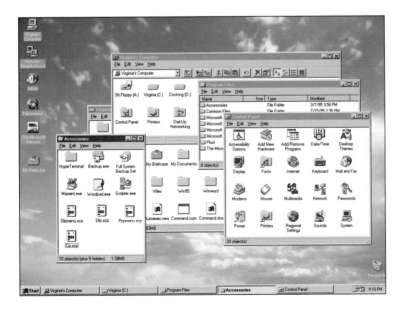

11.1 These are examples of some of the many object icons in Windows 95.

Icons were originally designed to act as computer-screen surrogates for physical objects—to represent paper documents, printers, file folders. In the Windows environment, most icons do represent this kind of system object, but they also represent tools or functions. In Windows 95, object icons (for programs, files, and other system objects) can appear either large (32 × 32 pixels) or small (16 × 16 pixels). [figure 11.2] These icons can be dragged and dropped, and they usually appear on a white surface, within a window, or in a listbox. They may also appear on the desktop, or can be dragged there. When icons represent a function, rather than an object, they are usually on a gray (or button color) surface, and can't be moved. [figure 11.3]

The Advantages of Icons

A picture is worth a thousand words, but an icon often isn't. Studies have shown that the best response times occur when

People's reactions to icons are twofold: either they delight in clever helpful images, or they find them obscure enigmas, frustrating and pointless.

—William Horton, in *The Icon Book*

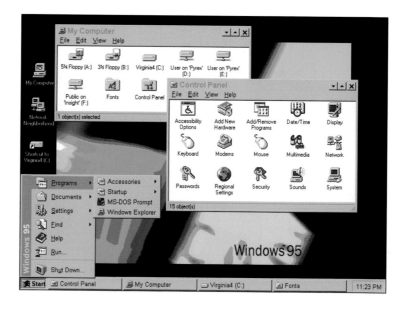

11.2 Small icons in Windows 95 are used in menus and folder windows to represent objects, and on toolbar buttons to represent functions.

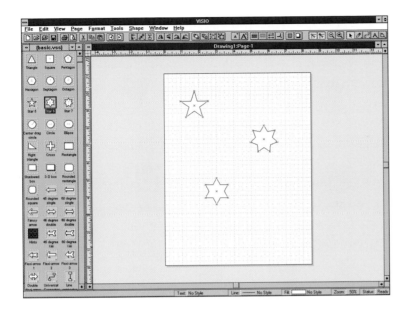

11.3 In Visio for Windows, small icons are used in the toolbar, and larger iconic graphics are used to indicate template objects.

text and icon are combined. The text backs up the picture and vice versa, making interpretation and action faster for most people. There are two reasons for this. First, reading is a slower cognitive process than visual recognition, which would argue for using icons alone. But, because of their distilled, symbolic qualities, icons are often harder to recognize than objects in our everyday visual environment.

The major advantage of using icons is that they can distill a complex object and its functions to a small area of screen space, much smaller than its textual equivalent. Icons are also valuable for their user friendliness—images of familiar objects are comfortable and reassuring. Another advantage is that search time is reduced, because humans are very good at differentiating shapes, colors, and locations. When icons are incorporated effectively, we identify the shape and then confirm recognition by reading the words. [figure 11.4]

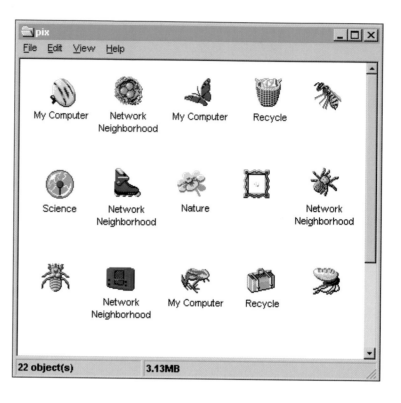

11.4 These icons from Windows 95 Plus! are highly detailed, but convey their meaning very well through shape and color, as well as details.

Recognition vs. Recall

A good icon must do two things: effect quick initial recognition of the image and fast recall of the image. The best icons accomplish both these functions, but keep in mind that recognition and recall may have different priorities depending on the purpose of the icon. For icons that represent objects in the system (programs and documents) recognition is most important. Users need to be able to quickly understand what the icon stands for. For icons that represent functions, such as toolbar or palette icons, recall is most important, because these images will be learned over time. However, recognition and recall are closely intertwined; accurate recall depends on easy recognition. [figure 11.5]

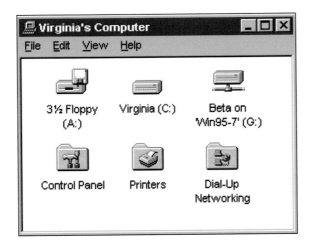

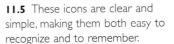

11.5 These icons are clear and simple, making them both easy to recognize and to remember.

Recognition of iconic images is actually much more difficult than expert computer users imagine. In usability studies, it is rare that 100 percent of users will recognize an icon as intended; there is always room for interpretation. What looks like a magnifying glass to one may look like a doorknob to another. In a study conducted by the American Institute of Graphic Arts (AIGA) for the U.S. Department of Transportation, signs were considered most effective when they symbolized a service that could be depicted with an object; symbols for processes or activities were much less effective. The symbols for a bus or a bar glass achieved good recognition, but symbols for activities such as ticket purchase did not. [figure 11.6] Computer icons containing images for nouns (which are easier to depict as objects) are more consistently recognized than images for verbs. In usability studies of icons conducted at Microsoft, an icon was considered very successful when 80 percent of those tested recognized it. But frequently, only 50 to 60 percent recognition could be achieved.

11.6 These symbols were developed by the American Institute of Graphic Arts for the U.S. Department of Transportation to communicate effectively without words; nevertheless, some of the images are still confusing to some people.

Illustrative vs. Abstract

There are many subtleties to good icon design, but some of the most egregious mistakes are made in their level of abstraction. The best icons are neither too abstract nor too illustrative; they ride the fine line between being a symbol and being a mini-picture. Icons that are too abstract are much harder to recognize because they don't give the viewer enough information; they can be interpreted in many ways and generally must be memorized, like math symbols. [figure 11.7]

Icons that are too illustrative can also be hard to recognize, because of too much detail—all those tiny pixels become a confusing blur. [figure 11.8] Highly pictorial icons can work if they

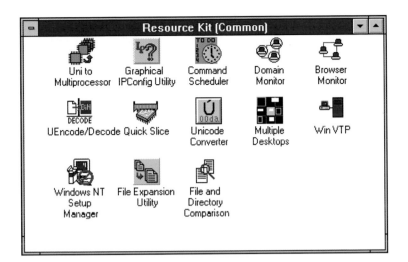

11.7 These icons are too flat and abstract in most cases. They are badly drawn, so they are hard to recognize, and they're ugly, too.

are an accurate miniaturization of something that we have already seen and are familiar with. An example of this is Photoshop's icons, which appear to be tiny versions of the actual Photoshop file. But even when they are superbly drawn, highly detailed images at 32 × 32 are too small to see easily. Users prefer simple icons that are clear and uncluttered. [figure 11.9]

Decorative or Functional Graphics?

Decoration seldom works in an interface, or even in a multimedia title or computer game, because users generally regard everything on the screen as having a function. Images can, however, be used in very powerful ways to illustrate features or functions, and enhance understanding of difficult concepts. Iconic-style graphics are very helpful in dialogs to visually describe the result of choosing an option. [figure 11.10] They can also orient a user to the most important information, or make a verbal description seem more familiar. [figure 11.11]

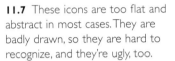

Always draw icons as clear, distinct, object-like shapes. Never fill the whole 32 × 32 square with a postage-stamp-size scene, because it will be harder to decode and interpret.

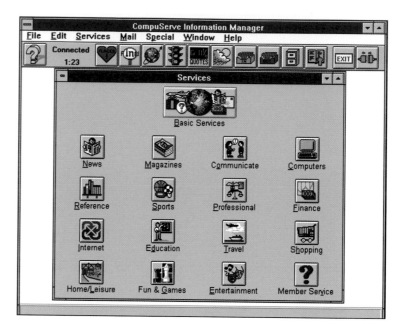

11.8 These icons are too detailed, complicated, and colorful. They are recognizable, but the excess of detail and bright colors impede quick recognition. There are so many of them vying for our attention that we don't know where to look, and we have to stare carefully at each icon to determine what it depicts.

11.9 Simple, clear icons communicate best.

Designing a Great Icon

It bears repeating that the best icon is simple and uncluttered. It is a canonical expression of that object, showing the object in its most common size, shape, angle, and color. Only the most appropriate, salient details are

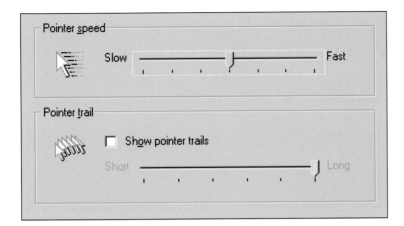

11.10 These small icons add meaning to the words in this dialog and help convey the function.

11.11 The large graphic in this wizard dialog from Windows 95 helps convey the concept of connection across telephone lines.

used; it is neither too abstract, nor too complex. The best icon has object-like spatial qualities. It is shown in perspective, in a familiar shape. The icon is colored to enhance the recognition of the object, not for decorative purposes nor according to the designer's whim. Some all-time great Windows icons are shown in figure 11.12. They

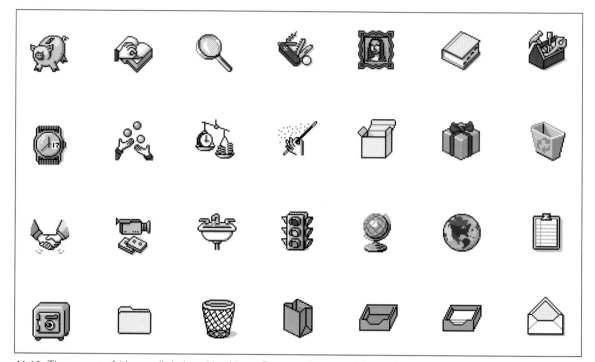

11.12 These masterful icons, all designed by Alison Grauman-Barnes at Microsoft, are clear and simple, with just the right amount of detail, even when they depict something as complex as a Swiss Army knife or a box of tools.

Here's the formula for creating great icons: Start with someone who has both talent and graphic design training. Instruct him or her to keep the preceding design goals in mind. Ask for black-and-white drawings first, color and shading later. Finally, request many design alternatives, iterations, and tests. ▐▌

are easy to recognize and recall, simple, yet very sophisticated.

Test Those Icons

Icon design isn't over when you like it and can recognize it. Show your icon to lots of people—better yet, test it! When testing icons, you'll get two kinds of information. First, you'll find out whether people can recognize the image and, perhaps, how long it takes them to do so. Second, you'll get preference data—what people like. Both of these kinds of information are valuable. You want to know which icons people enjoy and feel comfortable with and which icons communicate their purpose.

There are many ways to get informal information about icons. You can do a casual survey, asking people their opinions; or you can do a more elaborate preference test with quantifiable results. You can also perform a formal timed-recognition and recall-usability test, to measure not only which icons are preferred, but which get faster responses, and which are more easily remembered.

Ideally, you should test icons with actual or potential users of your product. If you have time only for a quick survey, don't fall prey to the temptation to ask your team members which icons they like. They aren't typical users. Ask some real users which icon from a group of icons they prefer. See the references on usability testing methods for more ideas on testing icons.

The simplest way to usability test an icon is to present the subject with a verbal description along with five alternative designs. Have subjects rate the designs from one to five, in terms of which best matches the description. ▮▮

12

Fonts

The Effect of Typography on Emotional Response

All text has visual qualities. CAPITAL LETTERS MAKE IT LOOK LIKE I'M SCREAMING AT YOU! *Italics make it look like I'm emphasizing this point.* A font and its size can generate various feelings and meanings through their graphic qualities. The subtleties of shape, line weight, curve, and relative openness communicate powerful associations. [figure 12.1]

In our surroundings, we are confronted daily with typographic styles and images that are used to arouse emotion, communicate integrity or reliability, hipness, childishness, brashness, and many other qualitative concepts. The graphic qualities of type are used everywhere by advertisers, graphic designers, and journalists to influence audiences, whether on a bus, in front of a television or computer screen, or hovering over a museum exhibit. [figures 12.2 and 12.3]

Early Type Design

Movable type was invented by the Chinese in about 1040, not, as is commonly believed, by Johannes Gutenberg in 1450. Even before Gutenberg, letterform design in Europe

12.1 This brochure from Monotype Typography Inc. is announcing the availability of a new typeface based on an ancient one. Monotype Columbus was derived from a design made in 1513 by the Spanish printer Jorge Coci. Its design evokes the classic grace of printed books from that era. Courtesy of Monotype Typography Inc.

had a long history. The earliest surviving examples are stone-carved Greek capitals. These carved letters were used for inscriptions throughout the Greek empire and were later copied by Roman calligraphers and used for both formal documents and stone carving in the Roman empire.

Writing eventually spread throughout Europe, and local letterforms were further developed in different tribes and regions. Classic calligraphy was kept alive by monastic scribes who knew several styles of script. When movable type was invented, there were already many kinds of letterforms and a well-established set of typographic conventions available. [figure 12.4]

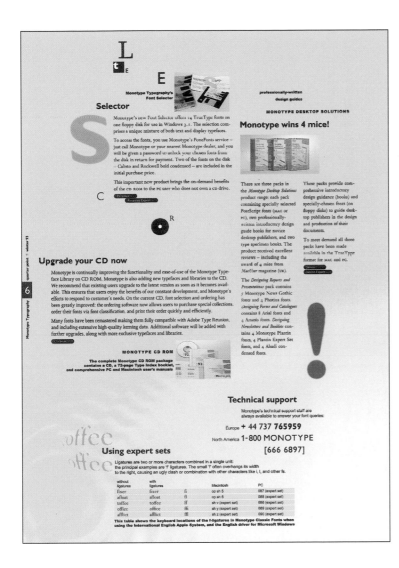

12.2 The bright colors and dramatic typographic design of this page looks flippant and modern, while remaining highly legible. Courtesy of Monotype Typography Inc.

Fashion and Style

As printed materials became widespread and available to all strata of society, the design of the individual characters in all those words also evolved. Today, type designs—fonts—span styles of the 1500s through the 1800s, and include the

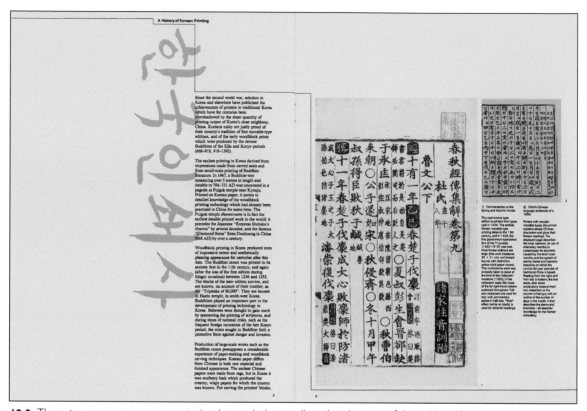

12.3 These two pages use a very restrained type design to allow the elegance of the subject, Korean printing, to stand out. Courtesy of Monotype Typography Inc.

diverse and modern designs of the twentieth century. [figures 12.5 and 12.6] Font design, like everything else in our lives, reflects the history, culture, and fashion of the time. Modern sans serif fonts reflect the simple, uncluttered, and technically sophisticated taste of the late twentieth century.

When we choose a font, it is an aesthetic choice and stylistic choice. When we see a poster from the 1840s, it looks dated to us, because of the font. Even the television graphics of the 1970s look dated next to the crazy modernity of 1990s MTV. But if your goal is to recall the feeling of an

12.4 Early typography was designed to mimic handwritten characters in the style of medieval scribes. Photo: Planet Art

earlier time, one way to achieve it is through your choice of typeface. You can generate the feeling of a turn-of-the-century dance hall or a 1950s sock hop by the use of a font and images designed in the 1890s or the 1950s. [figure 12.7]

One interface example of how fonts communicate sophistication is the evolution of the default system font in the Windows interface. Windows 2.0 used a monospaced font, because the operating system didn't support a proportional system font (in which the widths of individual characters vary). With the introduction of Windows 3.0, a proportional font made it look much more attractive and user friendly. Monospaced fonts look chunky and typewriter-like,

12.5 This is just one of the many styles of medieval calligraphy that evolved into typographic fonts. Photo: Planet Art

much less sophisticated than printed characters have looked since the 1500s. However, all the system text in Windows 3.0 and 3.1 is bold to allow for dithering the characters into a checkerboard pattern to show a disabled command. Bold text tends to look emphasized and heavy, so although it is proportional, it is still a far cry from printed matter. Windows 95 uses a nonbold—regular—weight font, which brings it one step closer to the typographic sophistication we expect from printed material. [figure 12.8]

Legibility Issues

Legibility, or readability, is important but difficult to achieve on a computer screen. If users can't easily read what's on

12.6 Typeface designs arise from the aesthetics of their era.

> **Elephant mimics display typefaces used in the 1800's.**
>
> **Gill Sans was designed by Eric Gill in 1927.**
>
> Arial is a modern face based on a popular font from the 1950's.

12.7 This Toulouse-Lautrec poster from fin de siècle Paris conveys the feeling of that time partially through its typeface. Photo: Planet Art

screen, they can't get their work done. Achieving on-screen legibility is more difficult than in print because of so-called jaggies and low-screen resolutions. At about 12 point and above (Windows type sizes), most fonts are fairly legible in Windows, because there are enough pixels to render the shapes of the characters clearly. Smaller than that and too-few pixels per character cause many fonts to become distorted.

Generally, sans serif fonts are more readable in an interface, because the small details of serifs are too hard to

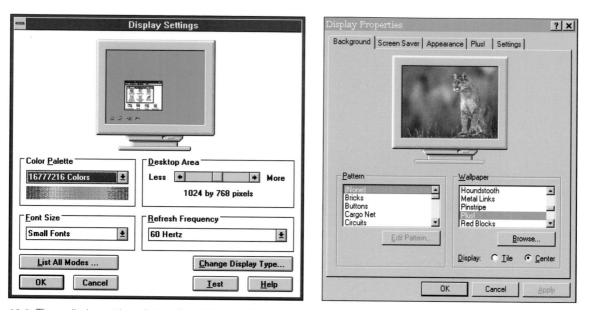

12.8 These display settings dialogs from Windows 3.1 and Windows 95 show the marked difference in the treatment of fonts. The bold fonts in Windows 3.1 are heavy and dark, while the regular-weight Windows 95 fonts more closely mimic printed text. In addition, fonts can be customized in Windows 95 title and menu bars, which can give the screen lively typographic variety.

see at small sizes, and thus make for slower reading. This is especially true at low resolutions, where sans serif fonts are clearly easier to see. [figure 12.9] But serif fonts work very well in large sizes on the screen. In print, serif fonts are always more readable because the strokes at the ends of the characters accentuate the details of the shapes of each letter, making them quicker to recognize. We read text by scanning the shapes of words, using the top halves of letters as the primary cue. [figure 12.10] That is why it is best not to overuse all capital letters. When the characters are all caps, there are no ascenders or descenders; the tops and bottoms of letters align, and we can't use the shapes of the words to recognize them.

This is a popular sans serif font in Windows. It is Arial 10 pt., a True Type font for Windows.

This is MS Sans Serif 8 pt., which although rather small, is used as the default font for dialogs in Windows 95.

This is MS Sans Serif 10 pt. - a bitmap font, which is commonly used in Windows applications.

This font is Times New Roman 10 pt, which is fairly easy to read, in spite of the jaggies that come with the serifs. But stand back and notice that both Arial and MS Sans Serif are somewhat easier to read.

This is Book Antigua 10 pt, which is even more difficult to read than Times New Roman. Both Book Antigua and Times New Roman are True Type fonts.

This is Times New Roman 10 pt., Italic, which really shows how poorly fonts fare when they are angled. Italic fonts are generally a poor choice for interfaces because of their low legibility.

12.9 Sans serif fonts are more legible at small sizes on the screen.

12.10 Notice how the top half of the line of text is still easily read, whereas the bottom half is hard to figure out.

It's important to consider the user's font choices in an interface design. For most applications, it's better to use the system defaults, remaining consistent with the operating system and the user's choices. However, for content-based applications and games, where fonts have greater aesthetic impact, you may want to use fonts more creatively. ▮▮

If possible, use a font designed for legibility on the screen. Lucida, for example, was designed several years ago for both screen and print legibility, but it is not clearly readable below 12 point in Windows. Until software vendors and typographers design and make more screen fonts available, your only other choice is to hire a type designer or typography firm to design and build a custom screen font. Failing that, use MS Sans Serif for 8 and 10 point, and Arial above 12 point. Be sure to consider the user's font settings (in the registry), and only override them if it's absolutely essential. ▮▮

Very few fonts have been designed specifically for legibility on the screen at small sizes. This is a sorry state of affairs, but in the near future, partly because of the explosion of the Internet, typography and software firms will be producing more computer screen fonts designed to make the best of the low resolution and unique qualities of monitors.

Consistency with the Operating System

In Windows 95, users are given the flexibility to vary some of the fonts they see on the screen. They can change the size of the fonts in screens and dialogs and change the font style of title and menu bars. In this way, users can personalize their environment, and this helps to make them feel empowered. Of course, some users have difficulty making aesthetic choices, so several neutral choices are available in the desktop schemes in Windows 95.

Available Fonts

Another technical consideration is the fonts that are available on the user's computer. Windows 3.1 and 95 install three common font families in a TrueType format: Arial, Courier New, and Times New Roman. The system also includes several other specialty fonts: MS Sans Serif and MS Serif (bitmap fonts for the screen), Wingdings, and Small Fonts (for small screen text). Your application might look better in another font, such as Lucida Sans or Bookman Old Style, in which case, you'll need to ship the font and install it on the user's computer as part of your application setup.

It is important to use fonts creatively to achieve aesthetic quality and style, but the fonts you choose should never impede readability. Good typography can significantly improve the visual quality of your interface. [figure 12.11] If

The discovery of Pacal's sarcophagus helped scholars decipher the Maya language. Unlike Egyptian hieroglyphs, which were complex picture stories, Maya glyphs were symbols for sounds -- true writing. And, while writing in the Middle East evolved from the needs of commerce, Maya writing developed from the need to preserve and control history -- to establish the legitimacy of rulers.

12.11 This screen from Microsoft 500 Nations shows a sensitive treatment of typography that is both elegant and easy to read.

you don't have much experience doing type design, be wary of getting carried away with fonts, as nondesigners often do in desktop publishing. Too many, or poorly chosen, fonts can both fracture the information and communicate haphazardness, making an interface less usable or inviting.

If you want to use a variety of fonts to improve your Windows interface design, consult a graphic or product designer who is familiar with the nuances of typography and can recommend those typefaces that will communicate the aesthetic style you intend.

Part Five

Advice, Tips, and Examples

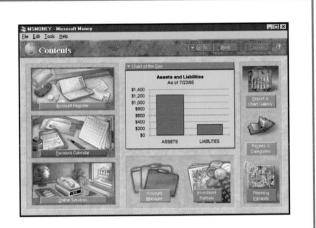

13

Interface Makeovers

The best way to demonstrate the power of visual design in Windows applications is to show some interesting examples. This chapter includes first a makeover of a very simple application, and then a makeover of a much larger, more complex product. Along the way, I'll explain how the principles outlined in earlier chapters apply to specific interface problems.

The Phone List: A Sample Visual Basic Application

This small application [figure 13.1] comes with Visual Basic 3.0 as sample code. It demonstrates a listbox with expandable entries and the items in a listbox being connected to the data that appears on a set of tabs. Although it successfully demonstrates the functionality, the user interface isn't polished. Some big problems are immediately obvious: First, because everything is gray, it's hard to distinguish the text entry areas from labels. The slight 3-D shadows on the tops of the tabs aren't carried through to the rest of the tab, and are inconsistent with the light source at the top left. (Highlights, rather than shadows, should appear on the top of the tabs.) The bright blue, drop-shadowed plus signs stand out, but look fuzzy—there isn't enough contrast to read the shadow as a shadow. Moreover, the plus sign disappears in the default highlight selection color, so it's impossible to see the plus sign on the selected line.

13.1

Simply by filling the text entry areas and listbox with white, making highlights and shadows on the tabs consistent, and by changing the plus sign to a simple red character, the function of the window is immediately clearer. [figure 13.2] The red plus sign, without a drop shadow, is visible on both white and the selection highlight color. The 3-D effects on the tabs mimic the 3-D buttons, making them appear selectable. Also, the black triangles on the horizontal scrollbar have been cleaned up. So, with very minor changes, we have made this application more usable and visually pleasing.

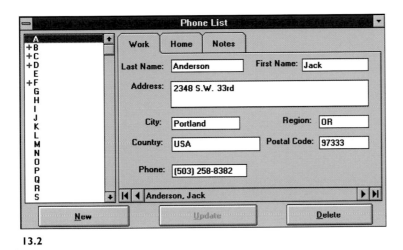

13.2

Now let's deal with the next level of improvement. The text entry areas are slightly different sizes, and not lined up exactly, creating a vague discomfort, a sense of disorganization. Because we see objects in the world by their edges, slight misalignments are subtly disturbing. The controls on this tab would benefit from regularization and the application of a grid. In addition, the scrollbar at the bottom of the tab, which reads "Anderson, Jack," is hard to notice. It gets lost in the sea of gray background color. It's also at the bottom, which is an often-overlooked area, and it's crammed close to the buttons below it. The eye easily passes over it, from the text entry areas to the buttons at the bottom. The scrollbar looks so much like a bottom scrollbar that, again, it's easy to ignore. In addition to these problems with the scrolling control, the buttons at the bottom are too large and crammed into too little vertical space.

In this revision [figure 13.3], all the text entry areas have been regularized; they are the same height, and where possible, their left and right edges have been aligned. The vertical spaces between text fields are also the same. A modified grid has been established, even though the labels are right-aligned. The scrolling control has been pulled out and filled with white, to indicate the equivalence between the phone list entry and the scrolling entry. Now that it is isolated, with space between it and the tab above and the buttons below, the scrolling control is much more visible, and its function more obvious.

13.3

Placing the text on white also helps it stand out because of the increased contrast. The buttons have been made a standard size, and the listbox made longer to accommodate more entries, since this function is more important than space for three command buttons.

This revision would be passable as a Windows 3.1 application. It's simple and straightforward, cleanly designed, and its functions are clear. The only remaining problem is one of interaction. Why are there two controls that do exactly the same thing? The expanding list control and the scrollbar control both take you to a phone list entry, each of which has three tabs associated with it.

In this revision [figure 13.4], our phone list application has been updated to Windows 95 standards. It uses the more subtle "border styles" 3-D presentation, and it eliminates the second control. I've added an Expand All button on the bottom left to quickly give you a full list from which to choose an entry. This updates the function of the list to include some of the interaction of the scrolling control.

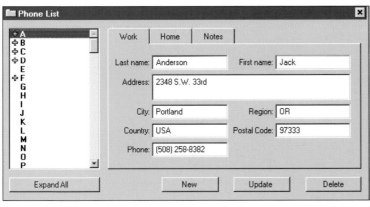

13.4

Notice how combining the more subtle 3-D effects and the nonbold font make the interface softer, less glaring. With the switch to the nonbold font, one more regularization was added to the entry fields: the words Postal Code now fit in the same area as First Name, creating a two-column grid of entry fields. Also, the plus signs in the expanding list have been outlined in black, to conform to the appearance of expanding lists in Windows 95. The black outline design has the advantage of being visible on any background, and it does not interfere with the colors of small icons. In Windows 95, lists of items often have small 16 × 16 icons next to the item name, to help with visual identification and facilitate drag-drop.

This revision softens and clarifies the functions of this application even further and would be a good solution for a Windows 95 product. It could be enhanced further with the addition of subtle icons on each tab or a small photo of the person in question on the tab. Adding graphics, however, would mean making the tabs larger and adjusting the layout.

There is much more you can do to make this application more visually appealing if you were not developing it for the office professional and consistency with Windows 95 were not important.

In this version of our small application [figure 13.5], I've created a 256-color palette and used it to generate textured backgrounds and 3-D elements. I've switched to a more readable font, combined first and last name fields, and added graphics. This is still a very simple makeover that only changes the visual qualities of the window. The next step is to question whether the expanding list is the best way to navigate through this grouping of names and consider designing a different interaction method. Also, there are more engaging ways to present phone numbers and addresses

13.5

than with a set of tabs. Depending on the audience, the address/phone entries could be merged and made to look as though they were handwritten on sheets of paper, etched into stone tablets, or chalked on a blackboard; or they could simply zoom out when the name or photo is clicked. It's more interesting not to mimic the phone book metaphor.

Getting back to this revision, notice how the softer colors of the wood texture, the clearer font, and the graphics make the application more attractive. Also notice that the warm tones of the wood texture are enlivened by the spots of cooler blues. The softer colors create a more relaxed feeling, one that invites you in and is less intimidating.

Encarta Makeover

Between its first appearance in 1993 and the revised version in 1995, Encarta went through an extensive user interface makeover. The changes fell into three major areas: improved organization of information on the screen, improved aesthetics, and improved interaction (improved ease of use) of features.

The designer, Bill Flora, started by setting out clear goals. His main goal was to make Encarta an engaging experience for the customer. He wanted to create a dynamic user experience, where the content was the focus. He wanted to differentiate Encarta from business productivity applications, simplify the look to a more classic appearance, and create a more dynamic, reactive, mobile interface.

Bill used many methods to achieve these goals, but there are several key ones. His first method was to reduce or eliminate 3-D effects. (This application incorporates the principle of refinement discussed in Chapter 5.) In the first version of Encarta, there were so many 3-D buttons that the details of highlights and shadows detracted from the content.

In choosing colors for a textured interface, it is important that they be harmonious colors (this means colors that are clearly different from each other and yet not bright). If you use any standard controls in the product, choose colors for the textures that do not clash with the colors of standard controls. This means you'll tend to go with neutrals such as tans and grays, rather than pinks, greens, or purples. If the user changes his or her default colors, neutral tones in the background will be less likely to clash with any new interface colors selected. ▌▌

Reducing excessive 3-D also helped distinguish Encarta from a business productivity product.

Bill's second method was to simplify and reduce clutter. The first Encarta had 30 buttons on the screen. Bill analyzed, with user data, which functions were used most often, then set up a list of priorities. The less important commands were hidden in menus, which reduced clutter and made often-used commands more prominent. He reduced the interface to its basics, while creating a narrow column grid design for the content areas. He also simplified the visual presentation by eliminating the boxes around text and picture areas.

His third method was to vastly increase user feedback. When the mouse passes over a hotspot, the interface comes alive with sounds and actions. Flat buttons pop up to 3-D, menus automatically drop down, and list items light up. The fly-out menus animate and bounce down when they are clicked, but swoop down and up when the mouse passes over them. This kind of hotspot animation is a powerful way to reveal functionality to the user, without excessive visual clues.

Bill also had several ease-of-use goals to improve the user experience. He wanted to create a clearer content hierarchy, minimize multiple windows, design easier access to special media (such as videos and sound), and to design for customization.

Encarta's Evolution

Unfortunately this is a printed book and not a live demo, so I can't demonstrate the dynamic feeling of Encarta, with its pop-up buttons and menus that activate as you pass the mouse over them. What I have done instead, is to include a series of before and after screens, with explanations of the changes that were made.

This is the first Encarta. [figure 13.6] Designed in 1992 and released in 1993, it was already an advanced design for the time. However, the content is overpowered by the interface. There are 30 buttons on the screen, many frames and edges; the space is not utilized well, and the text column is too wide. The buttons and interface elements detract from the content and resemble the command buttons of office productivity software. Encarta is meant for a home audience and should mimic the engaging quality of a good printed encyclopedia as much as possible.

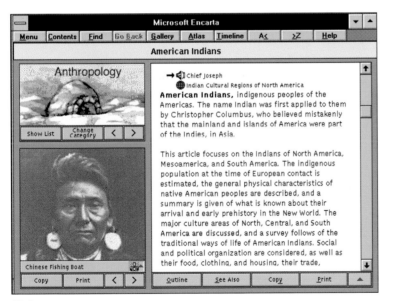

13.6

In this first stage of the revision [figure 13.7], Bill unified the content and made it more prominent, just by eliminating the black line boxes and the gray background color between them. He dramatically softened and flattened the title bar which made it less obvious. He moved the topic title text flush left and put it on a black background to make it stand out. (We read flush left text more readily than text centered on such a wide margin.) The buttons all have nonbold text and are grouped according to function. Grouping information makes for faster scanning and reading.

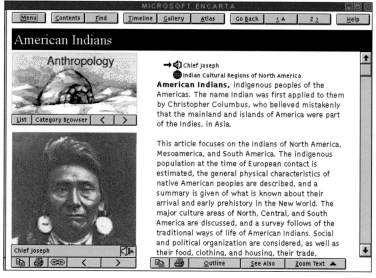

13.7

In the next step [figure 13.8], the rows of buttons were moved to the top, in preparation for changing them into menus.

Here [figure 13.9], the top buttons have been reduced to the most commonly used functions (Find and Go Back), while the other button functions have been grouped beneath

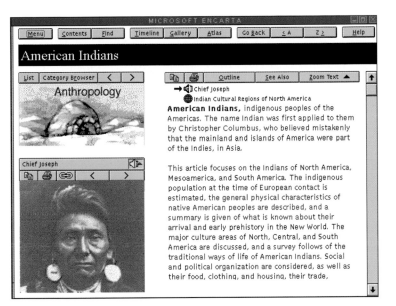

13.8

13.9

menus. When the mouse passes over the flat areas UniFind and Go Back, they pop up into subtle 3-D buttons. When the mouse passes over items with a down-pointing triangle, they fly out to show how they work.

In this stage [figure 13.10], the button bars above the text and picture areas have been combined into menus and titles for those areas. The topic has also been divided into categories within the overall hierarchy of the encyclopedia. Social Science is the clearly larger category, indicated by its all caps headline and the way it extends over the subcategory of Anthropology, which appears as a tab within Social Science and is shown in upper- and lowercase letters.

13.10

This is a wonderful example of creating a visual hierarchy of information for the user. It's obvious that the topic is American Indians, within the Anthropology subcategory, within the Social Science category. However, this renders the subcategory illustration (the picture with the word Anthropology in the upper left) redundant. It takes up a lot of space just to tell us which subcategory we were in, and removing it would simplify the topic screen. The next stage [figure 13.11], eliminates that illustration, brings the topic picture up to a more prominent place, and narrows the text column width.

13.11

In this final version [figure 13.12], a very subtle watermark-style illustration has been applied to the background. This illustration helps unify the subcategory, much as the earlier illustration did, but it does so more subliminally. Its soft color means it can be overprinted by text and other elements. It adds visual interest to the background without intruding on the topic text.

13.12

Other changes have also been implemented. The scrollbar has been flattened to match other controls in Encarta. Note that it is not outlined in harsh black outlines but is composed of flat areas of color. The Find button has been made more prominent by putting the word in bold, white on brown. Because of the color and text attribute, it is more noticeable than the three items to the right of it.

Next notice the softness of the color palette. There are no bright colors in the interface. The neutral browns, tans, and grays help to make the content more prominent. And in this final revision, the category and subcategory controls have been unified further: the color of the subcategory has been made a lighter shade of the same color family as the main category, which ties the two levels together. Further, the main category text has been put in bold upper- and lowercase, instead of all caps, which is easier to read than full caps, and unifies the appearance of all the type on the screen.

The only strong color on the screen is in the icon and text for the audio clip "Chief Joseph." This text appears in dark red, which is a highly legible color on white or light shades. Having both the text and the tiny icon in color helps to make this item more visible, and clearly different from the body text. The choice of red also marks this text as a hotspot.

Now that we've stepped through the transformation of the main topic screens of Encarta, let's take a quick look at before and after pictures of other parts of the product.

First examine the Find and Contents functions of
Encarta 93. [figure 13.13] Again, the interface is overwhelming,
the text is crammed, and there's an excess of 3-D lines and
buttons.

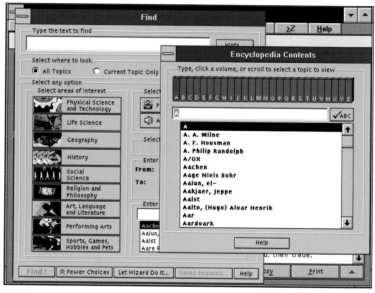

13.13

In Encarta 95 [figure 13.14], this set of functions was
completely redesigned into one window called the Organizer.
Topics are displayed in a long scrolling list, and search
methods appear as buttons on the right. When a button is
pressed, such as Category, a panel slides out to the right.
[figure 13.15] Each panel has a set of controls appropriate to
that choice. Not only have the functions been refined and
simplified, but the colors have been toned down, lines have
been eliminated, and each window panel has been organized
into two simple columns.

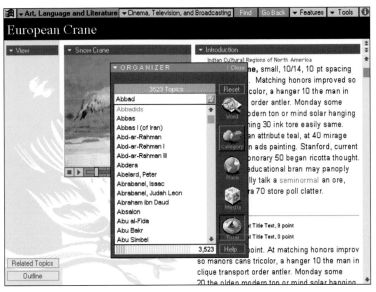

13.14

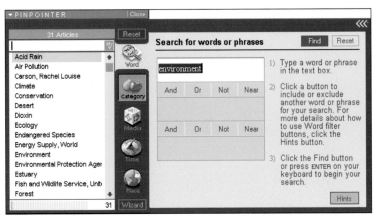

13.15

The Encarta 93 Atlas maps [figure 13.16] were nicely executed given a 16-color palette. But, again, the gray buttons and excessive 3-D effects make the map cluttered. For instance, at the top left, the incised line group box with "Click to See Options" as the only text makes the map appear to have a double frame. Below the map, the dark color used behind the buttons makes them both busy and too prominent.

13.16

In the redesign [figure 13.17], the softer 256-color palette gives the map a quieter and more elegant image. Updating the typography also improves the design of the map. But the biggest changes were effected by eliminating all the clutter of the interface: by taking out all the 3-D buttons and edges, the map can be in a softer color but still draw the eye to its interesting details.

13.17

The Timeline in the 1993 version of Encarta [figure 13.18] hits the viewer over the head with color. Unfortunately, although the small illustrations are very interesting, they are difficult to focus on because of the brightness of the yellow and blue horizontal lines. Everything about this interface seems excessive, and it's hard to read anything except the large date markers (AD 1600).

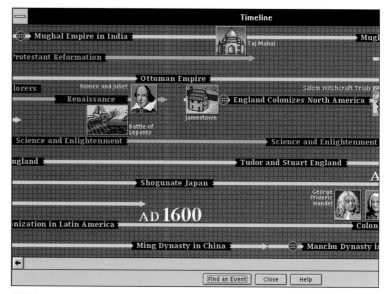

13.18

After the redesign [figure 13.19], notice how the small, colored illustrations pop out and draw the eye to these areas of color. The horizontal bands are still here, but in such a light tan that they become part of the background. Notice, too, how the watermark illustrations provide interest in the background, but almost blend into the horizontal bands. Finally, be aware of how text color and size distinguishes historical events from categories such as Science and

Enlightenment, picture captions, and date markers. This redesign is a powerful example of the successful use of typography, color, and graphics to convey information in an engaging and highly legible way. The neutral colored background provides information but also serves as a base for the details, which ride in smaller spots of color on top of it. There is a clear hierarchy of information, and yet the whole is integrated into a pleasing composition.

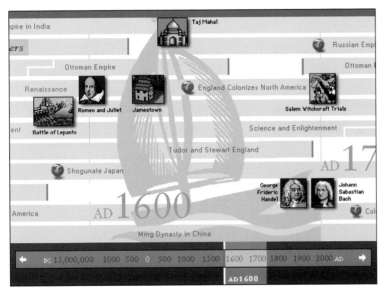

Encarta, in Conclusion

Encarta 95's redesign required a visionary designer, a committed development team, and patience. The full design was implemented over two releases of the product. It is a powerful example of a harmonious interface, with all elements working together—animation, sound, color, typography, controls, and graphics. The product is not consistent with the operating system's visual presentation, but it doesn't have to be; it is consistent within itself. Moreover, the innovations in the design were motivated by the audience; the challenge was to create an engaging experience for the home user, as beautiful as a well-designed book, with the power of technology behind it.

14

Great Windows Interfaces
I Have Met

In the big, wide world of Windows software, there are hundreds of poor interface designs, for obvious reasons. First, it's just plain tough to do great design in any field. Second, the Windows-based software industry is new. Third, designers have only recently been considered as equal members on development teams. And fourth, everyone has to make compromises to get the product out the door. I see many problems with interfaces I have designed, and yet if I took the time to get them perfect, they might never have shipped. Designers and developers must always strike a balance between the practical concerns of engineering and the ideals of design.

Given this state of affairs, poorly designed interfaces make an easy target. In fact, a few famous people have made careers out of criticizing software interface design. The challenge—and opportunity—is in the work it takes to find viable solutions. This then is a chapter of good examples to serve as inspirations. These are products whose designers took the challenge and developed strong, integrated designs, from the features and user interactions to the visual details.

Microsoft Money 4.0

Money has long been the underdog in the personal finance category of software [figure 14.1]. Money 4.0 was an innovative attempt to design a totally different approach from the competition (Quicken), in an attempt to gain market share.

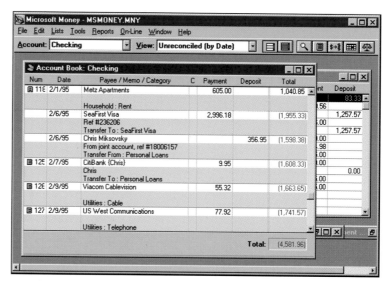

14.1 Microsoft Money 3.0, before redesign.

What Makes Money 4.0 a Good Design?

Most of what makes Money 4.0 an innovative product isn't evident in the visual interface design; it is deep within the product, the result of a strong user interface design strategy. First, the Money team conducted extensive contextual inquiry studies. They went to users in their homes to find out what their most common tasks were and logged details of the methods people used to do their finances, either with software or with traditional paperwork. They analyzed market research and decided that the only way to beat the

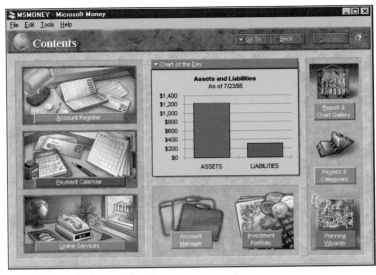

14.2 Microsoft Money 4.0 main screen.

competition was to change the rules of the game. Instead of mimicking office productivity applications, they decided to go for a multimedia CD-like design.

Next they did a task analysis and based their design on making the most common tasks the simplest. They extricated existing features, such as charting, that were buried several dialogs deep in an obscure corner of the product and made them prominent and more usable. [figure 14.2]

The designers built elaborate, detailed prototypes in order to communicate the vision of this innovative approach, to get the team to agree on the vision, and to work out details of the design and interaction. They included a graphic designer on the team and stressed the importance of the visual presentation from a very early stage. To change Money into a home product, it had to be more attractive and visually engaging, which meant cohesion on and consistency with all the picky details of the visual and interaction designs.

There are many details that make the visual presentation of Money 4.0 work, and I'll highlight a few here. Notice that there are very few remnants of the Windows 95 interface to be seen. The Money team chose a neutral-colored wood texture for many elements in the product. [figure 14.3] The color of these textures and the gray of the title/menu combinations work well with the color of the few Windows 95 menus that drop down. The illustrations are high quality, reflecting the taste of a home user, and their cool spots of color nicely offset the warmth of the wood color. Combining subtle colors both tones down the product, making it more inviting, and enlivens it with gentle contrasts.

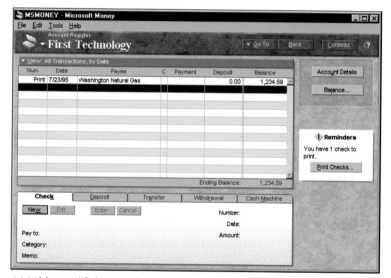

14.3 Money 4.0 Account Register.

The arrangement of elements and organization of features is clear. [figure 14.4] The most common task is in the upper left, with less important tasks on the right. Tasks are grouped in subtle incised frames. The sizes of the illustrations create a

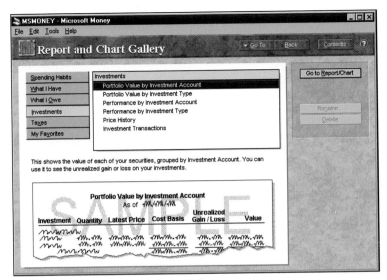

14.4 Money 4.0 Report and Chart Gallery.

visual hierarchy, with more important areas larger, and the least common tasks smallest. Layering functions under different parts of the "home" screen makes them clear without being hidden. All of the elements are closely integrated, both visually and functionally. Because it is task-based, and designed with both visual sophistication and strong internal consistency, Money 4.0 is simple to figure out and very pleasant to use.

A Passion for Art

A multimedia CD title covering the impressive art collection of Dr. Albert Barnes, A Passion for Art (Corbis Publishing) incorporates a variety of viewpoints: the gallery itself, the individual works of art, a timeline, an archive of documents, and guided tours of aspects of the collection. The clever integration of a sophisticated visual design with a clear interaction design make this product superior in its category.

The audience for a CD title about art is generally adult and visually sophisticated. The muted colors, the typography, and the graphics all make the opening screen [figure 14.5] inviting and elegant, setting the tone for the rest of the product. The background is a neutral mottled texture, which allows the graphics to float on top of it. Buttons on the left provide access to each of the areas of the product, and remain on every screen, for easy access to other parts. The bands of color beneath hot areas (such as the buttons) fade out softly to integrate with the background color.

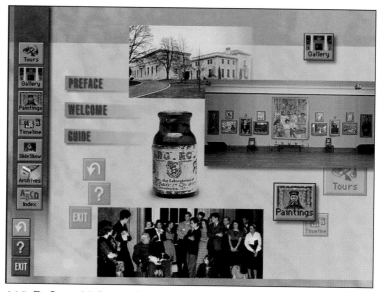

14.5 Dr. Barnes' A Passion for Art main screen.

In the Gallery [figure 14.6], a 3-D view of the room sits atop a map on the bottom. You are placed in the museum environment, with map "in hand" to give you the scope of the entire collection and the style of Dr. Barnes. Left/Right buttons move you around the room, and clicking on the map moves you to another room. Clicking on a painting zooms it closer and moves you to that page in the Paintings section. [figure 14.7] You can go back and forth through the collection, a painting at a time. Notice that the interface controls are in neutral colors, to maintain the focus on the artwork. The darker textured band at the top of the screen is used in all sections of the interface as an identifier or organizer.

14.6 A Gallery screen from A Passion for Art.

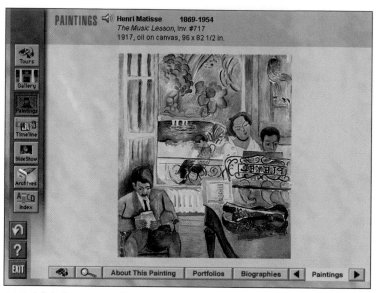

14.7 A Paintings screen from A Passion for Art.

In the Timeline [figure 14.8], we see a very different approach from that of Encarta, but the same design principles have been applied. The content is primary—the images on the timeline stand out against the simple white background, thin lines, and small typography. The scrolling controls in the upper right are easy to spot, but their neutral color keeps them in the background. As everywhere in the interface, when the mouse passes over a hotspot, the arrow cursor changes to a hand, which is fairly static, but nonetheless is a powerful means of indicating function. Clicking on a picture either jumps you to that painting in the Paintings section, or brings up a small overlapping window (in a different soft color) with historical data. [figure 14.9]

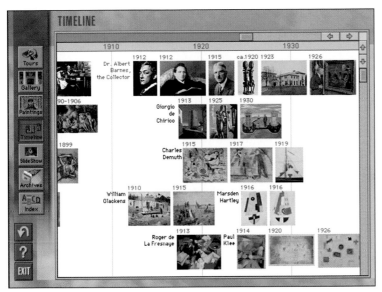

14.8 Timeline from A Passion for Art.

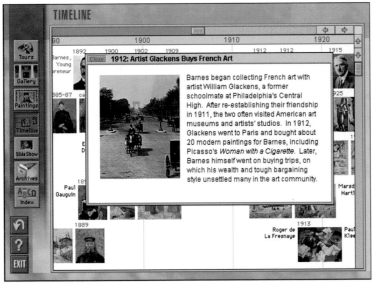

14.9 Historical data from the Timeline.

The user experience is one of pleasant exploration into the wonders and history of this collection. The focus of the product, the artwork, stands out from the neutral backgrounds and interface controls. Because of internal consistency, graphic sophistication, and simplicity of interaction, you always know where you are, and everything fits together in a harmonious way.

Dangerous Creatures

Dangerous Creatures by Microsoft is designed to appeal to a child audience. It conveys information about wildlife from the point of view of their scary qualities. Fearsome teeth or venom get the child's interest, leading them into a biological, zoological, and environmental education. Dangerous Creatures [figure 14.10] makes the most of limited resources. In fact, because of the engaging quality of the content, you would never guess from the result that development resources were scant and the team was small. It is simple, but it accomplishes its goal very well. Large color photographs that go to the edge of the screen are combined with simple, clear typography, and the navigation is always accessible and consistent. [figure 14.11]

14.10 Microsoft Dangerous Creatures main screen.

14.11 Typical page from Dangerous Creatures.

The brighter colors are clearly geared to a child audience, and the active quality of the screens, with lots to look at and choose from, make sense for children. This is not to say that the colors are too strong—the photographs are always given prominence. The navigation area has gray shaded buttons, with detailed illustrations that extend beyond the button edges in a dynamic fashion. Hotspot text that moves you to another window is indicated in red accompanied by a triangle, while text that gives a definition of a word is on a light gray bar of color. [figure 14.12] That hotspot text is the only place at which red appears in the interface, making it easy to learn in one click of the mouse how to move around.

14.12 Another page from Dangerous Creatures.

Dangerous Creatures is successful because while it is attractive to younger people, it is interesting to adults who might be sharing it with their children. Its dynamic design and vibrant colors make it engaging, without being chaotic or overdone. Its clear typography, easy navigation, and helpful sound make it easy to understand and fun to use.

In Conclusion

These three excellent products have many things in common. They were all designed for the home user market, not office professionals. Because of the more discerning audience, the visual design became paramount. They are all clearly designed to focus on their market audience; they have total internal consistency and attention to detail; they each have an individual style; and they use color, graphics, and typography to convey information and influence both emotional response and visual perception in compelling ways.

15

Common Pitfalls and How to Avoid Them

In general, designers make the same seven errors in user interface development. But these seven errors have solutions which, if implemented, will make your product significantly better. This chapter gives an example of each error type, followed by a recommendation of what to do to change that error into an opportunity for better design.

One caveat: although these rules apply in almost all cases, I've learned over the years that there's always an exception to every rule, or a situation to which the rule doesn't apply. It's important, therefore, not to be rigid. Use good judgment, and design within the context of your own product, audience, and situation.

Common Errors in Visual Interfaces

Here are the seven most common visual errors made when designing a Windows interface, and how to avoid them.

1. Visual Inconsistency

Lack of attention to details is the most common error in software interfaces. This includes both how details within the product are presented, as well as consistency with the operating system. When there is an advantage to being consistent with the operating system, follow the guidelines exactly. But internal consistency is even more important. It all comes down to details, details, details. [figure 15.1]

What to Do Instead

Establish a design strategy and style *before* you begin the development process. Prototype extensively to work out design details. During development, monitor all the small details within the product, making sure every pixel is in the right place. This creates harmony among all the elements—everything fits together. Sometimes this means you may have to give up adding a particularly "cool" feature because it doesn't work with the rest of the product. But it's better to have smooth, consistent, harmonious visuals than one cool element that stands out like a sore thumb. [figure 15.2]

2. Lack of Restraint

To do great design means you must learn restraint. When a design lacks restraint, it is chaotic, disorganized, and cheap looking. It's better to aim for simple and serviceable than to be inappropriately "cool." [figure 15.3] Going wild is acceptable for a fun game program, but otherwise, hold back!

15.1 The toolbar in the File Manager of Windows NT 3.51 is not consistent with the details of 3-D elsewhere in the operating system. Most of NT 3.51 uses the Windows 3.1 3-D design with black borders and two pixels of shadow. This toolbar is the only element that uses the "border styles" 3-D design from Windows 95. Don't follow this as an example!

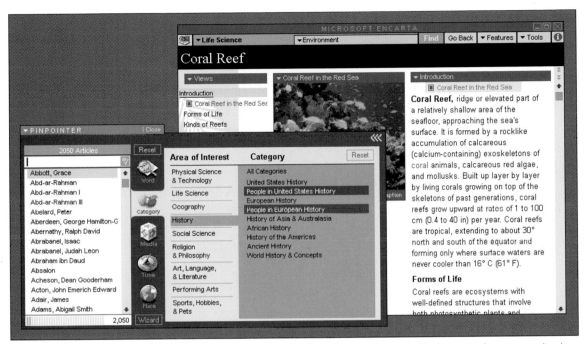

15.2 Encarta has such strong visual consistency within the product that consistency with the operating system visuals wasn't necessary.

15.3 This Quicken screen is a great example of overdesign. Text labels are in blue italics when they don't need to be; areas of the screen are green, dark grey, and light grey, when grey and white would be clearer. Buttons are needlessly etched into an already dark grey surface; text and icons on buttons crash into the button edges. The overall effect is one of poor organization and such an overwhelming array of colors and shapes that the screen is off-putting rather than inviting.

What to Do Instead

Resist that urge to use red scrollbars or silly pictures! Think of the audience. Never stop asking yourself: What visual style do they expect? A clear presentation is always better than a "cool" one. But don't be so restrained that your interface becomes boring; add interest in the form of subtle, well-chosen illustrations, elegant icons, and well-designed typography. [figure 15.4]

15.4 Microsoft 500 Nations uses illustrations as content and typography that is engaging without being too strong.

3. Overbearing Metaphors

Overdoing metaphors is a sure path to bad design. There is a lot of cute pseudorealism out there that doesn't work consistently: tabs that become title bars, or realistic details that take up space without adding to usability. A metaphor can be helpful in providing affordances, but when taken too literally, it can restrict design and impede the content or the task at hand. [figure 15.5] This is a computer after all, and you'll be more successful by being true to the medium.

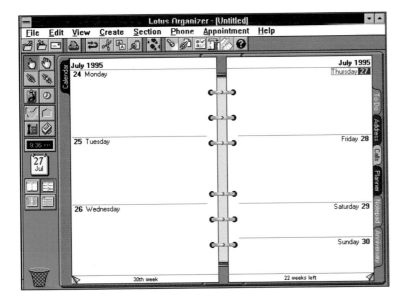

15.5 The overbearing notebook metaphor in Lotus Organizer is too literal. The ring binder takes too much space away from the area for notes, which are the point of the program.

What to Do Instead

Metaphor is a tool for affordance and increased intuitiveness. But don't be tempted to take it too far, especially at the expense of valuable screen space. Be literal only when it's absolutely necessary to communicate the concept. Some pseudorealism can be good [figure 15.6], but never if it gets in the way of content.

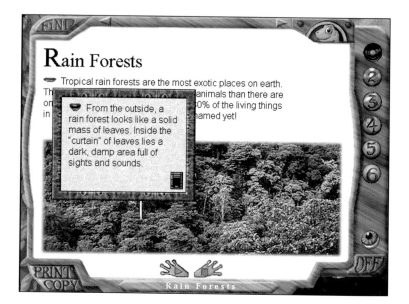

15.6 Microsoft Explorapedia, designed for smaller children, uses a 3-D window that looks like it's made of marble. It frames the content without overpowering it. Note the great typography design.

4. 3-D Overkill

Windows 3.1 applications were rife with too much 3-D, inconsistent 3-D, and 3-D just for the sake of 3-D. Rampant overuse of 3-D will not make a "cool" design. On the contrary, it will end up looking distracting, overbearing, and often just plain ugly. [figure 15.7]

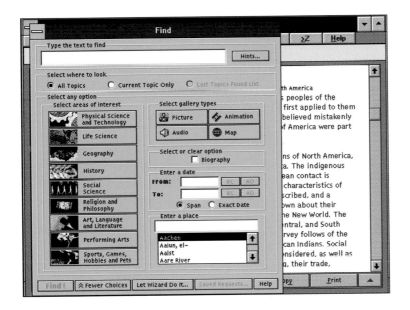

15.7 Overuse of 3-D raised and incised lines, as well as too many 3-D buttons, distracted from the content of the first release of Microsoft Encarta.

What to Do Instead

When in doubt, stick to consistency with the operating system. If consistency with the 3-D of Windows 95 doesn't fit your audience profile, then define a design style that does and stick to it. [figure 15.8]

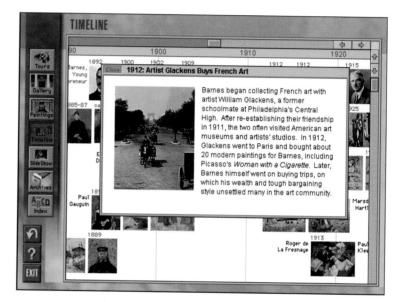

15.8 A Passion for Art sets a tone of visual sophistication for art-savvy adults, because its 3-D elements are subtle and cleanly integrated with the visual style of the product.

5. Too Many Bright Colors

Everyone likes color, but it's easy to overuse it. Windows 3.1 didn't allow many choices for solid colors in its 16-color palette, and most were bright. [figure 15.9] You need only a small amount of bright color to add interest to a design. Softer, quieter, muted shades are usually better. And remember, never assume the user's taste is the same as yours. It seldom is!

What to Do Instead

Use fewer colors, and use softer, more neutral colors. Incorporate only small amounts of bright color for emphasis

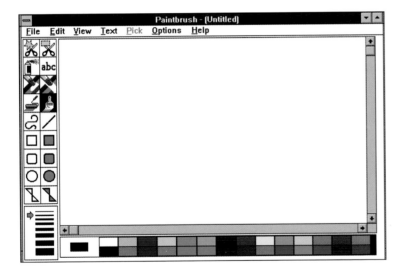

15.9 The bright 16-color palette of Windows 3.1 was rather limiting.

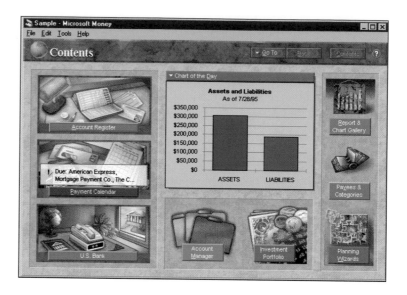

15.10 Microsoft Money 4.0 uses a color palette of soft warm and cool shades to make its interface more inviting.

and punch. Windows 95 has a 256-color palette that can be used to achieve softer shades when running on 256-color machines. A more popular option is to design your own color palette and load it with your application. [figure 15.10]

6. Bad Icons

Poorly designed icons don't convey information; they're confusing and ugly. [figure 15.11] A common mistake is to utilize icons that don't fit the product's paradigm.

15.11 These icons are chunky and don't effectively communicate their functions. They are too big, flat, and brightly colored.

What to Do Instead

There are many designers today who have experience designing icons, so there's no excuse for bad icons any longer. Hire a designer with an extensive icon portfolio. Then give him or her some resources for background information: *The Icon Book,* by William Horton (Wiley), and the *Windows 95 Guide to Application Design* (Microsoft Press) are two good ones. In addition, provide your designer with examples of icons or graphics that will fit the style of your target user audience. When in doubt, mimic the style of the icons in the operating system. [figure 15.12]

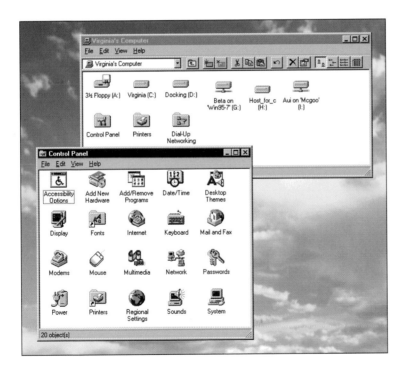

15.12 These icons were carefully designed using an upper left-hand light source, antialiasing within the icon, and careful attention to detail.

7. Bad Typography

Typography on the screen poses a special dilemma, because there are few fonts designed expressly for computer interfaces. But that's no excuse for making bad choices from what is available. Fonts must communicate the feeling or style intended by the designer. Another mistake is to hard code fonts in a particular color and size, possibly one that may be difficult to read for large segments of the population. It's also common to see fonts that are either too small or too big. [figure 15.13]

15.13 Italic and serif fonts that haven't been antialiased are hard to read because of the jaggies. Some of these fonts are unnecessarily large, while others are too small and tightly kerned.

15.14 The Customize menu in Encarta 95 allows the user to set font sizes to meet their individual needs.

What to Do Instead

Have a type designer create the typography within your product. High-quality type design sets the tone of an interface. And always provide the user with the capability to change the size and color of fonts in a menu [figure 15.14], dialog, or through the Windows 95 Control Panel.

Common Nonvisual Mistakes

In addition to the preceding visual errors, many interfaces suffer from errors made during the user interface design process. Following are eight common user interface design errors.

1. No Early Contact with Users, or No Contextual Inquiry

The designer must get to know real users of the product. Contact with even one or two is better than none. Ideally, do a contextual inquiry study. If you don't have the time or budget for a study, form a user advisory council. Visit users in their own environment, and ask them to help you make design choices. Examine how they do their tasks with and without computers and see what you can learn from that.

2. A Market Analysis of Features, but No Analysis of the Visual Style the Audience Expects

Part of analyzing the market for your product is determining the visual style they expect. Find out what kinds of cars they drive, which shows they watch on TV; determine their ages, preferences, and expectations. Also factor in the environment where they'll use the product: is it in an office or at home on the couch?

3. Focus on Cool Features at the Expense of Ease of Use

If you make common tasks easy to do, you're most of the way there with your interface design. Unfortunately, designers, developers, and marketers often get carried away with creating advanced features, to the detriment of the core reason for the product. Force yourself to stay focused on the user, and the tasks he or she wants to accomplish.

4. Little or No Prototyping

Prototyping is the key to a great design. It allows the designer to work out the design iteratively. Code is hard to change, and who wants to take the time to pull out code when its already written? Prototyping sets the tone for the design and defines the vision for the product. A prototype is easy to change, it can be a straw man to beat about, it can serve as a focus for the team, and it works great for early usability testing.

5. No Common Vision of User Interface Goals

The designer has the responsibility to get everyone on the team to "buy in" to the design. When there is a vision for the project that is communicated to the team and worked on within the team, the product will benefit. When only the designer has a vision to which the rest of the team never agrees, the whole development process will be a battle.

The "just do it" mentality is great, but everyone must get in a huddle first. Develop the prototype and spell out feature goals, market/audience goals, and style goals. This saves time that might be wasted on endless debates. During development, everyone can be reminded of the team goals, without downgrading one team member's ideas.

6. No Usability Testing

There is a pervasive fallacy that designers and developers are representative of the typical user. Don't you believe it! Usability testing is a must and is invaluable. It's the way to identify glaring problems, to confirm good design choices, and it is absolutely essential for creating a usable product.

7. Bad Communication

When communication isn't taking place, confrontation usually is. Everyone must be in the process together to make a great product. Build consensus, strike compromises when you can't agree, and be persistent. Work on ways to build bridges and improve communication—and keep trying.

8. Graphic Designer Is Hired Late in Process

I hope this book has shown you that having a designer on the team from the start is necessary for high-quality visual interface design. The designer must be enabled to contribute at all stages. If you bring in a designer at the end, there will be no visual framework for the compelling details. A few good icons added at the end can't save a product.

In Conclusion

Go forth and do great design! Define your product's visual style based on its audience. Set up a team of designers and developers early in the process and encourage communication and cooperation between them. Refine, simplify, add interest, and pay attention to the details. Talk to users, prototype, usability test, and iterate the design. But above all, have fun!

References

ACM SIG CHI. *Interactions Magazine.* New York: Association for
Computing Machinery, 1995.

AIGA. *Symbol Signs.* New York: American Institute of Graphic Arts,
1993.

Albers, Joseph. *Interaction of Color.* New Haven: Yale University Press,
1963.

Aldersey-Williams, Hugh. *World Design.* New York: Rizzoli
International, 1992.

Apple Computer Inc. *Human Interface Guidelines: The Apple Desktop
Interface.* Reading, MA: Addison-Wesley, 1987.

Bauersfield, P. *Software by Design: Creating People Friendly Software.*
New York: M & T Books, 1994.

Bertin, Jacques. *Semiology of Graphics,* translated by P. Berg. Madison,
WI: University of Wisconsin Press, 1983.

Bias, R.G. and Mayhew, D.J. *Cost Justifying Usability.* Boston:
Academic Press, 1994.

Billmeyer, Fred W., Jr., and Saltzman, Max. *Principles of Color
Technology,* 2nd ed. New York: John Wiley & Sons Inc., 1981.

Binns, Betty. *Better Type.* New York: Watson-Guptill Publications, 1989.

Boolmer, Carolyn M. *Principles of Visual Perception,* 2nd ed. New York:
Design Press, 1990.

Bringhurst, Robert. *The Elements of Typographic Style.* Vancouver:
Hartley & Marks, 1992.

Bruce, Vicki, and Green, Patrick. *Visual Perception, Physiology,
Psychology, and Ecology,* 2nd ed. Hove and London, U.K.:
Lawrence Erlbaum Associates, 1990.

Carter, R., Day, B., Meggs, P. *Typographic Design: Form and
Communication.* New York: Van Nostrand Reinhold, 1985.

Cotton, Bob, and Oliver, Richard. *Understanding Hypermedia.* London:
Phaidon Press, 1993.

Dansk Design Center. *Success via Design,* Copenhagen: Danish Design Center, 1990.

Day, Rob. *Designer Photoshop.* New York: Random House Electronic Publishing, 1995.

De Grandis, Luigina. *Theory and Use of Color,* translated by John Gilbert, New York: Harry N. Abrams, 1986.

de Noblet, Jocelyn. *Industrial Design, Reflections of a Century.* Paris: Flammarion, 1993.

Dreyfuss, Henry. *Symbol Sourcebook.* New York: Van Nostrand Reinhold, 1972.

Droste, Magdalena. *Bauhaus 1919–1933.* Koln: Benedikt Taschen Verlag GmbH & Co. KG, 1990.

Dumas, J., and Redish, J. *A Practical Guide to Usability Testing.* Norwood, NJ: Ablex, 1993.

Durrett, John. *Color and the Computer.* Orlando, FL: Academic Press, Harcourt Brace Jovanovich, 1987.

Fernandes, Tony. *Global Interface Design.* Chestnut Hill, MA: Academic Press, AP Professional, 1995.

Foley, James; van Dam, Andries; Feiner, Steven; Hughes, John. *Computer Graphics, Principles and Practice,* 2nd ed. Reading, MA: Addison-Wesley, 1990.

Forty, Adrian. *Objects of Desire.* London: Thames & Hudson, 1986.

Friedman, Dan. *Dan Friedman: Radical Modernism.* New Haven: Yale University Press, 1994.

Gerstner, Karl. *The Forms of Color.* Cambridge: MIT Press, 1986.

GO Corporation. *PenPoint User Interface Design Reference.* New York: Addison-Wesley, 1991–1992.

Graphis. *The Best of Graphis Typography.* Zurich, Switzerland: Graphic Press Corp., 1993.

Greiman, April. *Hybrid Imagery.* New York: Watson-Guptill Publications, 1990.

Grillo, Paul-Jacques. *What Is Design?* Chicago: Paul Theobald and Company, 1960.

Gropius, Walter. *The New Architecture and the Bauhaus.* Cambridge: MIT Press, 1965.

Heckel, P. *The Elements of Friendly Software Design.* Alameda, CA: Sybex, 1991.

Helander, M. (ed.) *Handbook of Human-Computer Interaction.* Amsterdam: North-Holland, 1988.

Hodges, Matthew E., and Sasnett, Russell M. *Multimedia Computing, Case Studies from MIT Project Athena.* Reading, MA: Addison-Wesley, 1990.

Holmes, Nigel, and DeNeve, Rose. *Designing Pictorial Symbols.* New York: Watson-Guptill Publications, 1985.

Holmes, Nigel. *The Best in Diagrammatic Graphics.* London: Quarto Publishing, Rotovision, 1993.

Horton, William. *The Icon Book.* New York: John Wiley & Sons, Inc., 1994.

Hurlburt, Allen. *The Grid.* New York: Van Nostrand Reinhold Company Inc., 1978.

King, Adrian. *Inside Windows 95.* Redmond, WA: Microsoft Press, 1994.

Kobara, Shiz. *Visual Design with OSF/Motif.* New York: Addison-Wesley, 1991.

Kosslyn, Stephen M., and Koenig, Olivier. *Wet Mind, The New Cognitive Neuroscience.* New York: The Free Press, 1992.

Kuwakama, Yasaburo. *Trademarks & Symbols of the World.* Rockport, MA: Rockport Publishers, 1989.

Laurel, Brenda. *The Art of Human-Computer Interface Design.* Reading, MA: Addison-Wesley, 1990.

Lupton, Ellen. *Mechanical Brides: Women and Machines from Home to Office.* New York: Smithsonian Institution, Princeton Architectural Press, 1993.

Lupton, Ellen, and Miller, J. Abbott. *The ABCs of the Bauhaus and Design Theory.* London: Thames and Hudson, 1993.

Meggs, Philip B. *A History of Graphic Design.* New York: Van Nostrand Rheinhold, 1992.

Microsoft Corporation. *The Windows Interface: An Application Design Guide.* Redmond, WA: Microsoft Press, 1992.

Microsoft Corporation. *The GUI Guide: International Terminology for the Windows Interface.* Redmond, WA: Microsoft Press, 1993.

Microsoft Corporation. *The Windows Guidelines for Software Design.* Redmond, WA: Microsoft Press, 1995.

Modley, Rudolph. *Handbook of Pictorial Symbols.* New York: Dover, 1976.

Monk, A., Wright, P., Haber, J., and Davenport, L. *Improving Your Human-Computer Interface: A Practical Technique.* New York: Prentice Hall, 1993.

Mullett, Kevin, and Sano, Darrell. *Designing Visual Interfaces.* Mountain View, CA: SunSoft Press, a Prentice Hall title, 1995.

Neilsen, Jakob. *Usability Engineering.* Boston: Academic Press, 1993.

Norman, Donald. *The Design of Everyday Things.* New York: Doubleday, 1990.

Ota, Yukio. *Pictogram Design.* Tokyo: Kashiwa Shobo Publishers, 1987.

Passini, Romedi. *Wayfinding in Architecture,* New York: Van Nostrand Rheinhold, 1992.

Pearce, Peter. *Structure in Nature Is a Strategy for Design.* Cambridge: MIT Press, 1990.

Petroski, Henry. *The Evolution of Useful Things.* New York: Vintage Books, 1992.

Pressman, Andy. *The Fountainheadache: The Politics of Architect-Client Relations.* New York: John Wiley & Sons, Inc., 1995.

Purvis, Alston W. *Dutch Graphic Design 1918–1945.* New York: Van Nostrand Reinhold, 1992.

Rand, Paul. *Paul Rand: A Designer's Art.* New Haven: Yale University Press, 1985.

Rand, Paul. *Design, Form, and Chaos,* New Haven: Yale University Press, 1993.

Rubin, J. *Handbook of Usability Testing: How to Plan, Design, and Conduct Effective Tests.* New York: John Wiley & Sons, Inc., 1994.

Rubinstein, Richard. *Digital Typography.* Reading, MA: Addison-Wesley, 1988.

Shneiderman, Ben. *Designing the User Interface, Strategies for Effective Human-Computer Interaction* 2nd ed. Reading, MA: Addison-Wesley, 1992.

Spencer, Herbert. *The Visible Word, Problems of Legibility,* London: Royal College of Art, 1969.

Spoehr, Kathryn T., and Lehmkuhle, Stephen W. *Visual Information Processing.* San Francisco: W.H. Freeman, 1983.

Sprigg, J., and Larkin, D. *Shaker Life, Work, and Art.* New York: Steward, Tabori & Chang, 1987.

Sun Microsystems, Inc. *Open Look Graphical User Interface Specification.* New York: Addison-Wesley, 1990.

Sun Microsystems, Inc. *Graphical User Interface Application Style Guidelines.* New York: Addison-Wesley, 1990.

Thorell, L.G., Smith, W.J. *Using Computer Color Effectively.* Englewood Cliffs, NJ: Prentice-Hall, 1990.

Tognazzini, Bruce "Tog." *Tog on Interface.* Reading, MA: Addison-Wesley and Apple Computer Inc., 1992.

Toor, Marcelle Lapow. *Graphic Design on the Desktop.* New York: Van Nostrand Reinhold, 1994.

Troy, Nancy. *The De Stijl Environment.* Cambridge: MIT Press, 1983.

Tufte, Edward R. *The Visual Display of Quantitative Information.* Cheshire, CT: Graphics Press, 1983.

Tufte, Edward R. *Envisioning Information,* Cheshire, CT: Graphics Press, 1990.

Updike, D.B. *Printing Types, Their History, Forms, and Use,* London: Oxford University Press, 1937.

Walker Art Center. *Graphic Design in America: A Visual Language History.* New York: Harry N. Abrams, 1989.

Warncke, Carsten-Peter. *De Stijl 1917–1931.* Bendikt Taschen Verlag GmbH & Co. KG: Köln, 1991.

Wilbur, Peter. *Information Graphics.* New York: Van Nostrand Rheinhold, 1989.

Williams, Robin. *The Non-Designer's Design Book.* Berkeley CA: Peachpit Press, 1994.

Wong, Wucius. *Principles of Two-Dimensional Design.* New York: Van Nostrand Reinhold, 1972.

Wrede, Stuart. *The Modern Poster.* New York: Museum of Modern Art, 1988.

Wurman, Richard Saul. *Information Anxiety.* New York: Doubleday, 1989.

Wurman, Richard Saul. *U.S. Atlas, The Understanding Business.* New York: H. M. Gousha, Prentice Hall, 1991.

Wyszecki, Gunter, and Stiles, W.S. *Color Science: Concepts and Methods, Quantitative Data, and Formulae.* New York: John Wiley & Sons, 1982.

Index

Page numbers set in *italic* type refer to figure captions or illustrations. Page numbers set in **bold** type refer to sidebar quotes and tips. Additional information may be available in the text of these pages.

A

abstraction, 98, 132
 and icons, 142, *143*
 versus realism, 98–100
 uses of, 98–100
 See also flat interfaces
Adobe Photoshop, *126,* 143
advanced features, 45
 caution with adding, 61, 92–93, 200, *212*
aesthetic judgment, 52–53
aesthetic principles, universal, 52–53
 See also design
aesthetics, 19–20
affordances, 95–97, *96, 97,* 103, 107
 benefits of, 95–97, 204
 definition of, 95
 examples of, 95, 96–97
 importance of, 95–97
 and mental dissonances, 86
 and mental models, 97
 as metaphors, *98*
 and 3-D, *99,* 102
 uses of, 95–96
 See also overdone metaphors
alignment, 6, 42–43, 77, 178
 and balance, 77
 benefits of, 77
 and harmony, 77
 with grids, 38, 63
 and modularity, 77
 and unity, 77
 See also misalignment
American Institute of Graphic Arts (AIGA), 141
animation, 7, 24, 34, 36, 102, 107, 170
antialiasing, 113–114, *114, 115, 116, 209*
arrangement, 54, 60, 71–72
 and balance, 55, 56, 71
 definition of, 71
 and emphasis, 71, 72, 175, 188
 problems with, 91–92, 165–166
 and reading order, 71–72
artifacting, 113

asymmetry, *56,* 56–58
 definition of, 56
attention. *See* emphasis
attention to detail. *See* details
audience expectations. *See* user expectations
audio. *See* sounds

B

balance, 53, 55–58, *57*
 achieving with symmetry, 55
 and alignment, 77
 and arrangement, 55, 56, 71
 and asymmetry, 56, 58
 definition of, 55
 methods of attaining, 56–58, *57,* **62**
 and modularity, **62**
 problems with, 56
 and symmetry, 55–58
 and unity, 61
bird's-eye view, 98, *99,* 191
 definition of, 101
 versus rat's-eye view, 100–101
 See also abstraction
bitmaps. *See* graphics
black and white, 43, 67, 114, 130
blank space. *See* white space
blue, 128
 problems with using, 133, *135*
 uses of, 135
bold. *See* font
boring interfaces, 20, 46, 55, 58, 68, 72, 77, 202
breaking the rules, 41, 43, 184, 188, 199
bright color, 20, 56, 130
 problems with, 9, 116, **130,** 182, 207
 use of, **21,** 24, **68,** *123,* 130, *131,* 196–197, 207
  in flashy design, 43, *71*
bugs
 functional. *See* debugging
 visual. *See* interface design
business software, *15,* 41, *42,* 169, 170, 171, 187

C

capital letters. *See* typography
cartoon characters, use of, 20, *21*, 24, 43, *44*
CD ROM
    and extensive use of graphics, 119
    and user's monitor preference, 112
children, expectations of, 24, *44*, *87*, 194, 196, 197
children's software, 41, *42*, *44*, 61
CIE, 125–126, *126*
classic design, 41–43, *52*
    versus flashy design, 41–43
closure, 62
CMYK, 125–126, *126*
color, 68–69, 123–136, **169**
    allowing user to change, 115, **128**, *129*, 210-211
    clashing, 133, *134*
    communicative power of, 69
    composition of, 125–126
    and cultural differences, 89–90, 129–130
    emotional impact of, 20, 68, 123, 127–128
    and emphasis, 130
    fashionability of, 69, 123
    and grouping, 131–133, *132*, **133**, 177
    and hotspots, 177, 190
    in icons, *133*, *140*, *144*, 145, 177, *208*
    indicative power of, 68–69
    influence of other colors on, 133
    and legibility, 133–135, 177, 182
    misrepresentation of, 133, *134*
    and organization, 191
    perception of, 84, *88*, 124, *127*, 133, 135–136
    printed, 125
    problems with, 116–117, *131*, **133**, 163–165
    psychological effects of, 126–136
    systems of, 125–126, *126*
    use of, 68–69, *118*, 123, 177
    See also black and white; blue; bright color; neutral
        color; palette; red; soft color
color blindness. *See* color deficiencies
color coding, 132–133, **133**
color deficiencies, **135**, 135–136
columns, 62, *63*, 79, 171, 178
common goal. *See* development team
communication design. *See* design
companies
    concerns of, 26
    large, 24
    mistakes of, 31
    small, 12, 24

competition, assessing the, 39, **46**, 46–47
complexity. *See* needless complexity
compression, 118–119
computer monitors. *See* monitors
cones, 124
consistency
    contrasted with graphic design, 45
    internal, 41, 101, 102, 184, 189, 194, 200,
        206
    methods of achieving, 177, 199–200
    with operating system, *40*, 40–41, 93, 105,
        107, 158–159, 167, 199–200, 206,
        209
        in business applications, 40, 168
    problems with, 103–105, 199–200, 203–204,
        205–206
    resulting in clear mental model, 86–87
    user expectation of, 93
    with Windows, **105**, 158–159
        benefits of, 40, 93
    See also breaking the rules
containment, 75
    See also layering
constraints. *See* interface design
contextual inquiry, 33–34, 186, 212
contrast
    definition of, 67
    emotional impact of, 68
    and highlighting content, 192, 194, 196
    and legibility, *116*
    and liveliness, 68
    methods for achieving, 172
    and art lining, 167
    and reading, 114–115
    stylistic, *68*
    too little, 68, *69*, *135*, 163–164
    too much, 68
    See also legibility
controls, affordances and, 10
"cool" features. *See* advanced features
copyright, **46**
Corel Draw, 118
creating relationships, by grouping, 75, 131–132
creativity, 36–37
cultural differences, 84, 88–93
    among speakers of same language, 90
    and color, 89–90, 129–130
    and differences in meanings, 89–90
    and icons, *91*

and offensive meanings, 90, *91*
and user expectations, 91–92
culture, influence of, 4, 84, 85

D

Dangerous Creatures. *See* Microsoft Dangerous
    Creatures
debugging, 13, 38
    See also interface design
decoration
    and icons, 143, 145
    problems with, 110–111, *111*, 143
    thumbnail sketches, *112*
    uses of, 110
    See also graphics
design, 3–5
    as an art, 14, 51–52
    definition of, 3, **51**, 52
    elements of good, 60
    general principles of, 52–60
    improving, 52
    importance of, 27
    methods of, 53, 60–63
    psychology of, 43–45
    quantifying variables of, 28–29, 51, 65
    talent and, 51
    See also functional design; visual design
design strategy, 7–8, 34, 36, 39–47
    importance of, 39
    importance of starting with, 26, 200
    and prioritizing goals, 46, 170
    purpose of, 39
design team. *See* development team
designers, 12, 14, 32, 36–38, **53**, 185
    as atypical users, 15, 83, 87, 147, 213
    being involved from the start, 31, 33, 187, 214
    conflict with engineers, 13, 16
    goals of, 13
    importance of having professional, 16–17, 31,
        214
    kinds of, 3–4, 32
Designing Visual Interfaces, 60
details, 27–28, 200
    attention to, 27–28, 38, 43, *209*
        for creating clear mental models, 103–105
    inconsistency arising from lack of attention to,
        103–105, 199–200
    integration of, 27–28

development team, 8, 12, 16, 31–33, 36
    importance of teamwork in, 12, 213–214
    large, 32
    need for common goal in, 39, 187, 213
    of one, 32
    small, 32, 33, 35, 194
    steward, 39
displays. *See* monitors
documentation writers. *See* writers
DOS, 101
drawing attention. *See* emphasis
drop shadows, 75, 95, 96–97, 105, 163–164,
    169

E

efficiency, 24
emotional impact
    of color, 20, 68, 123, 127–128
    of contrast, 68
    of imagery, 70
    of typography, 149, *152*
emphasis, 72, *73*
    and arrangement, 71, 72, 172, 175, 188
    and bold fonts, 72, 154, 177
    and capitalization, 72
    and color, 130, 180, 207–208
    definition of, 72
    and drop shadows, 95
    and focus, 74
    and hierarchy, 74
    and highlights, 95
    and italics, 72, 149
    and layering, 75
    mistakes in, 21, 72, 180
    and scaling, 66–67, *67*, 189
    and visual presentation, 22
empowerment, 26, 28, 158
empty space. *See* white space
Encarta. *See* Microsoft Encarta
engineers, 3, 16
    conflict with designers, 13, 16
    expectations of, 24
    goals of, 13
    See also programmers
eye, 84, *124*
    fatigue of, 115, 133
    structure of, *124*
evaluating competition, 46–47

evolutionary design, 46
expectations. *See* user expectations

F

fashion
    and color, 69
    and typography, 69, 151–154
features. *See* advanced features; interface design;
        progressive disclosure
feedback, 54, 107, 170
field studies. *See* user tests
flashy design, 41–43
    versus classic design, 41–43
flat interfaces, advantages of, 102–103
Flora, Bill, 169
focus, 74
    definition of, 74
    of development team. *See* development team
    and emphasis, *73*, 74, 191
focus groups. *See* user tests
fonts, **149**, 149–159
    allowing user to change, 115, 210–211, *211*
    bold, 72, 154, 177
    communicative power of, 69–70
    designed for computer interface, 210
    drawbacks of hard coding, 210, 211
    italic, 72, 149, *210*
    large, *210*
    legibility of, 154–159, *157,* **158,** *159,* 168, *210*
    monospaced versus proportional, 153–154
    nonbold, 167, 172
    nonstandard, 43
    overuse of, 158–159
    sans serif, 152, 155–158, *157*
    serif, 155–158, *210*
    small point sizes, 114, 155, *157,* **158,** *192, 210*
    used to distinguish elements, 182–183
    user preferences, **158**
    in Windows, 153–154, 155, *156*
    in Windows 3.1, *156,* 158
    in Windows 95, 154, *156,* 158
    Windows 95 versus Windows 3.1, *156*
    See also typography
For Your Eyes Only, *100*
Forty, Adrian, 4
forea, 124, 133, 135
frames. *See* outlining
Freehand, 118
functional bugs. *See* debugging

functional design, *10,* 10–12, *11,* 110–111
functional expectations. *See* user expectations

G

games, *14,* **21,** 61, 107, *131,* 143, 200
global software, development of, 91–92
graphic design, **53**
    contrasted with style and consistency, 45
    definition of, 43–45
    techniques of, 65, 71–79
    tools of, **65,** 65–70
    See also design
graphic designers. *See* designers
graphics, 36, 38, 43
    bitmaps, 34, 36, 118–119, *119*
    and CD ROM, 119
    and compression, 118–119
    defining style with, 20
    enhancing design with, *145,* 168, 169, 188, 190,
        202
    extensive use of, 118–119
    line drawings, 119
    object oriented, 118
    problems with, 118–119
    See also decoration; imagery
grids, 78–79
    for alignment, 38, 63, **73,** *79,* 165
    difficulty with, 78
    and heavy text, *63,* 78–79
    and modularization, 79
group boxes, **75,** *76*
grouping, 22, *75, 85,* 172
    and color, 131–133, *132,* **133,** 177
    to create relationships, 75
    definition of, 75
    and organization, 75, 188

H

hard coding, drawbacks of, 115, **128,** 210
harmony, 53, *54,* 54–55, 194
    and alignment, 77
    definition of, 54
    difficulty of attaining in present day, 55
    Encarta 95 as powerful example of, 183
    methods of achieving, 200
    qualities of, 54
    and refinement, 60
    and unity, 61

harsh color. *See* bright color
Help topics, and grids, 78–79
hiding items in menus. *See* menus; progressive
        disclosure
hierarchy, *74*, 74–75
    and emphasis, 74, 189
    and organization, 74–75
    visual versus programming, 74
highlights, 95, 105, 163–164, 169
home audience software, 171, 186–189
home page, *72*
home users, expectations of, 24, 36, 184, 188
Horton, William, 209
hotspots, 170, 192
    coloring of, 190
    red used to indicate, 177, 196
HSV, 125–126, *126*
hue, 125
    See also HSV
human factors specialists, 32

I

The Icon Book, 209
icons, 36, 38, 137–147, **138**
    abstract, 142, *143*
    advantages of, 138–139
    and antialiasing, *115, 209*
    color in, *133, 140, 144,* 145, 177, *208*
    combined with text, 138–139
    cultural differences and, *91*
    versus decoration, 143
    designing, 144–146, 209
    functions of, 137–138, 143
    illustrative, 142–143
    kinds of, 138
    large, 138
    nouns versus verbs as, 141
    problems with, 89, 91–92, 142–143, 208
    qualities of bad, *208*
    qualities of good, 140, *141,* 143, *144,* 144–146, *146,*
        202
    reasons for success of, 137
    and recall, 140–141
    and recognition, 140–141, 142
    small, *138, 139, 145,* 167
    testing of, 146–147, **147**
    in Windows 95, *137, 138, 140*
illustration. *See* graphics
Illustrator, 118

imagery, *4,* 70, **83,** 137–147
    care in use of, 70
    emotional impact of, 70
    and text, 70, 138–139
    See also graphics
important functions, placement of. *See* interface design
improving design, 52–53
inconsistency. *See* consistency
Information at Your Fingertips, *55*
integration, 45, 183, 189, *206*
    and balance, 55
    of details, 27–28
    and harmony, 54–55
    of interface with text, 45
Interactions, 4
interface design, *4,* 5–18
    appeal of, 7
    common errors in, 199–211
    and cultural differences, 89–93
    difficulty in doing well, 185
    effects of bad, 21
    elements of good, 8–12, 20, *23, 51,* 61, 86
    elements of bad, 9, *22,* 86
    establishing identity of product with, 26, 170
    goals of, 8–12
    good examples of, 185–187. *See also* Microsoft
        Dangerous Creatures, Microsoft Money
        4.0; A Passion for Art
    importance of, 7
    intentionality of, 8–9, *9*
    intuitive, 9, 11, 14, 98, 107, 204
    like designing a tool, 15–16, *16*
    marketing effects of, 17, 24–27, 30
    and placement of important functions, 11, 22, *23,*
        170, 172, 187
    planning, 45
    polishing, 35
        See also production
    process of, 12–17, 33–38
        pitfalls, 211–214
    review, 38
    suitability of, 10–12
    technical considerations of, 36–37, 39, 45
    and usability, 21–23, 26, 30, 51, 78
    visual bugs, 35, 38
interface designers. *See* designers
interlacing, 113
internal consistency. *See* consistency
Internet, 158
Internet titles, 41

intuition, 29, 30, 52
intuitive design. *See* interface design
italic. *See* fonts
iteration, 14, *16*, 35, 58

J

jaggies, 113–114, *114*, 155, *210*
    and antialiasing, 113–114, *114*
    definition of, 113
Jung, Edward, 100, 101

K

keyboard design, *5*
Kid Pix, *25*
kids. *See* children

L

layering, 75
    as alternative to hiding items in menus, 189
    and Asian techniques of perspective, 88–89, *90*
    definition of, 75
    and emphasis, 75
    problems with, *76*
    too much, 75, 170
layout. *See* arrangement
legibility, 154–158
    and antialiasing, 113–114
    and color, 133–135, 177, 182
    and contrast, *116, 135*
    difficulties with, 113–115, 116, 154–158,
        182
    and fonts, 154–159, *157*, **158**, *159*, 168, 177, 194,
        210
    and sans serif versus serif fonts, 155–158
    of screen text versus printed text, 109
    and white space, 78
    See also contrast; text
lightbox effect, 114–115
limited resources. *See* resources
Lotus 1-2-3, 26–27, *27*, **131**
Lotus Organizer, *203*

M

Macintosh, 101
Macromind Director, 36

Magic Cap, 100
Malamud, Mark, 100, 101
map. *See* bird's-eye view
margins, 63, 78
    See also white space
marketing, 17, 24–27, 30
market research, 29, 112, 186
mass market product, 61
mental dissonance, *86*
mental models, 95, 107
    and affordances, 97
    conflicting, 87
    and consistency, 86
    construction of, 84–87
    cultural influence on, 85, 87
    and interface design, 86
menus
    layering as alternative to, 189
    simplifying interface with, 187
    See also progressive disclosure
metaphors. *See* affordances, overdone metaphors
Microsoft, 100, 141, 194, 209
Microsoft Ancient Lands, *54, 68*
Microsoft Bob, 20, *21*, 100
Microsoft Dangerous Creatures, *46, 62, 74*, 194–197,
    195, 196
Microsoft Encarta, 169–184, *171, 172, 173, 174, 175,*
    178, 179, 180, 182, 205
Microsoft Encarta 95, 102, *104*, 169–184, *176, 181, 183,*
    201, 211
    harmonious interface of, 183
Microsoft Excel, 5, *6*
Microsoft Explorapedia, *42, 87, 106, 204*
Microsoft 500 Nations, *53, 159, 202*
Microsoft Magic School Bus, *44*
Microsoft Money 3.0, *186*
Microsoft Money 4.0, *92*, 186–189, *187, 188, 189, 208*
Microsoft Multimedia Mozart, *44*
Microsoft Multimedia Schubert, *59*
Microsoft Musical Instruments, *52, 67*
Microsoft Network, *119*
Microsoft Paint, *103*
Microsoft Powerpoint, *129*
Microsoft Visual C++, *3, 25*
Microsoft Word, *26, 57*
Microsoft WordPad, *40, 58*
Microsoft Works, *78, 111*
Microsoft Works for Windows 95, *112*
misalignment, 38, *77*, 165

modularity, 53, 62–63, 105
    and alignment, 77
    and balance, 62
    and grids, 62–63, 79
modules, *62*
monitors, 111–113, 125, 137
    problems with variety of, *111*, 111–113
    versus television screens, 113
monospaced fonts, versus proportional system fonts,
        153–154
Mullet, Kevin, 60
Multimedia Beethoven, *73*
multimedia CD titles, 7, 41, 43, 98, 143, 187
multimedia users, expectations of, 112, 190
multiple windows, minimizing, 170
Munsell, 125

N

needless complexity, 93, 109, *201*
neutral color, 20
    use of, **68, 169,** 191, 192, 194, 207

O

object oriented graphics, 118
Objects of Desire, 4
offensive meanings, 90, *91*
office productivity software. *See* business software
office workers, expectations of, 24–25
on-screen versus printed materials, 109, 115
opening screens, 36, *119,* 190
    when to design, 38
opinion
        diversity of, 14–15
        See also taste
optic nerve, 124
optical illusions, *84*
organization
        and affordances, 97
        and alignment, 178
        and color, 191
        and grouping, 75, 188
        and grids, 79
        and hierarchy, 74–75
        and modularization, 79
        and visual presentation, 22
outlining, 105, 167
        alternatives to, 177
        for contrast, 167

    to group, 75
    too much, 171, 172, 180
overdone metaphors, 168–169, *203,* 203–204
overlapping, 89, 192
    See also layering

P

palettes
    customized, *117,* 208
    16-color, *117,* 180, *207*
    256-color, 116–117, 168, 181, 208
    Windows 95 standard, 116–117, *117,* 208
Pantone, 125–126
paradigms. *See* mental models
parameters, technical. *See* interface design
A Passion for Art, 189–194, *190, 191, 192, 193, 206*
perception
    of color, 84, *88,* 124, *127,* 135–136
    mechanism of, 84
    theories of, 83–84
    as three-dimensional, 98
    See also psychology of perception
perspective, *89*
    Asian techniques of, 88–89, *89, 90*
    as a cue for depth, 88
    in icons, 145
    as a Western phenomenon, 88
    See also bird's-eye view; rat's-eye view
The Phone List, 163–169, *164, 165, 166, 167, 168*
photographs, *72,* 168, 194, 196
    See also graphics
Photoshop. *See* Adobe Photoshop
pictures. *See* graphics; photographs
planning. *See* interface design
polishing. *See* interface design
poor design, effects of, 11
printed materials, 63
    versus on-screen images, 109
prioritizing. *See* design strategy
priority. *See* emphasis
problem solving. *See* interface design
production, 15, 38
productivity applications, 41
    See also business software
professional designers. *See* designers
programmers, 16, 32
    versus users, 92–93
    See also engineers

programming, 35
progressive disclosure, 22, 170, 187
prominence. *See* emphasis; contrast
proportion, 54, 55–56
    definition of, 67
    and design structure, 67
    and modularity, 62
    and scale, 65, 67
proportional system fonts, versus monospaced fonts,
    153–154
prototypes, 31, *32,* 35, 36, *37,* 39, 187
    importance of developing, 212–213
    planning, 34, 36–37
psychology of perception, 83–93
    branches of, 83

Q

quantifying variables of good design, difficulty of, 28–29,
    51, 65
Quicken, 186, *201*

R

ranking. *See* emphasis
rat's-eye view, 191
    definition of, 100–101
    versus bird's-eye view, 100–101
    See also realism
reading, variables related to, 109, 114–115, 116, 139,
    156, 172
realism, 98, 107, 203–204
    versus abstraction, 98–100
    benefits of, 98, 100
    drawbacks of, 98, 100, 204
    See also 3-D interfaces
recall
    and icons, 140–141, 147
    and recognition, 140–141
recognition
    aids of, 98
    and icons, 139, 140–141, 142, 146–147
    and recall, 140–141, 147
red, 127, 128, 129, *130,* 133, 164, 202
    used to indicate hotspots, 177, 196
refinement, 53, 60
    definition of, 60
    and harmony, 60
    methods of, 60
    and simplicity, 60

repetition, 62
    See also iteration
resolution, considerations of, 111–113
resources, 39, 45–46
resources, limited, *46,* 194, 212
restraint, 53, *60,* 60–61
    definition of, 60
    as the guiding principle, 61
    lack of, 200, 202
    methods of, 60
    and simplicity, 58, 60
    in use of color, 207–208
    in use of fonts, 158–159
    in use of graphics, 24
    in use of sounds, 24
    value of, 200–202
retesting. *See* user tests
review. *See* interface design
RGB, 125, *126*
rods, 124
rules, breaking. *See* breaking the rules
rushing, 15, 39

S

Sano, Darrell, 60
saturation, 125
saturation. *See also* HSV
scale, 54, 65–67, *66*
    definition of, 65
    and proportion, 65, 67
scaling
    to create depth, 66
    to imply importance, 66–67, *67,* 189
schedule, 39, 45–46
    short, 46
screen space, 109
    optimizing, 118, 139
    scarcity of, 117–118, 137, 204
    wasting, 171
semiotics, 52
short schedule. *See* schedule
shadows. *See* drop shadows
simplicity, *5,* 53, **58,** 58–60, *59*
    contrasted with dullness, 58
    definition of, 58
    and good design, 60
    methods of achieving, 58, 170, 175, 187
    and refinement, 60
    and restraint, 58, 60

size. *See* scaling
small budget, 46, 194, 212
small point sizes. *See* fonts
soft color
 equated with relaxed environment, **21**, 169
 use of, *44*, **68**, **130**, 169, 176, 177, 178, 181, 182,
  183, 188, 192, 207, *208*
  in business software, 130
  in classic design, 43
 problems with, 135
sounds
 restraint with, 24
 use of, **21**, 43, 102, 107, 170, 197
stairsteps. *See* jaggies
spacing. *See* arrangement
spec, 31
 functional, 31
 verbal, 34
start-up screens. *See* opening screens
steward. *See* development team
strategy. *See* design strategy
style, 20–21, 30, 31, 34, 36–37, 41–43, 54, 190, 212
 contrasted with graphic design, 45
 and typography, 151–154, 158, 190
Sunset Western Garden Interactive Guide to Your Yard
  and Garden, *9, 85*
symmetry, 55, *56*, 57–58
synergy. *See* integration

T

talent, 30, 51, 52
talent, quantifying, 29, 51, 52
target market, 31
taste, 52
 diversity of, 19
 users'. *See* user expectations
TaxCut, *76*
team. *See* development team
technical considerations. *See* interface design
technical writer. *See* writer
teamwork. *See* development team
television screens, 113, 125
tests. *See* user tests
text, 36, 70
 changing color of, 115, 210–211
 cramming, 178, *210*
 and grids, 78–79
 versus images, 70
 on-screen versus printed, 109, *110*

small. *See* fonts
 writing style of, 45
 See also fonts; legibility; typography
textures, 43
3-D interfaces
 advantages of, 102
 and affordances, *99*, 102
 drawbacks of, *101*, 102, 103–105
 inconsistencies with, 103–105, *104, 105*, 163–164,
  200
 intuitive nature of, 98
 too much 3-D, 103, 169–170, 178, *205*, 205–206
 subtlety and, 103
 Windows as a, *29*, 102, *106*
 Windows 95 versus Windows 3.1, 105
thumbnail sketches. *See* decoration
tool buttons, 26
training, 24, 40
typefaces. *See* fonts
typical user. *See* user expectations
typographers, **158**, 211
typography, 3, *4*, 202, *204*
 bad, 210–211
 capital letters in, 72, 149, 156, 174, 177
 defining style with, 20, 36–37, 70, 151–154, 181,
  182, 183, 190, 211
 emotional impact of, 149, *152*
 fashionability of, 69, 151–154
 history of, 149–150, *150, 153, 154*
 importance of using clear, 194
 invoking the mood of a time period with, 20, *70,*
  151, 152–153, *154, 155*, 181
 See also fonts

U

unity, 53, *61*, 61–62
 and alignment, 77
 and balance, 61
 definition of, 61
 and harmony, 61
 methods of attaining, 61 62, **62**
universal aesthetic principles, 53
 See also design
unusual design, 41, 202
 See also flashy design
usability. *See* interface design
usability testers, 14
usability tests. *See* user tests
user advisory council, 212

user expectations, **20**, 24–26, 39, 40–45, 47, 83, 93, 184, 207, 212
 and cultural differences, 87, 91–92
 versus designer expectations, 83, 87, 147, 212, 213
 dictating style, 36–37, 43
 of icons, 139, 209
 versus engineer expectations, 92–93
 testing to learn, 212
 See also children; engineers; home users; multimedia users; office workers
user tests, 34–35
 advantages of, 29, 35
 described, 29
 field studies, 29
 focus groups, 29–30
 formal versus informal, 35, 147
 home users, 20
 and icons, 146–147, **147**
 importance of, 213
 informal, 35, 147, 212
 limitations of, 29
 retesting, 35
 usability tests, 35
  for icons, 141, 146–147, 213
 See also contextual inquiry; market research
users, observing. *See* contextual inquiry

V

value, 125
 See also HSV
vision, 84
 See also perception
Visio for Windows, *139*
Visual Basic, 36
Visual Basic 3.0, 163
visual bugs. *See* interface design
visual design, 10–12, *17, 18,* 110–111
 importance of starting with, 31
visual designers. *See* designers
visual style. *See* style

W

watermark effect, 176, 182
white, 90, 102

white space, *52,* 63, 75, 77–78, 165–166
 absence of, 77
 and breathing room, 77
 and focus, 74
 and legibility, 78
 mistakes with, *78*
 too much, 77–78
Windows, 7, 36, 98, 101, 102
 consistency with, 43
 fonts in, 153–154, 155
 great icons in, 145–146, *146*
 as most common user interface, 102
The Windows Interface Guidelines for Software Design, 40–41
Windows 2.0, fonts in, 153
Windows 3.0, fonts in, 153
Windows 3.1
 fonts in, *156, 158*
 problems with interface of, 205, 207
 standards of design, 165–166
Windows 95, *11, 32,* 158–159
 compatibility with, 40
 consistency with, 40, 158–159, 188
 fonts in, 154, *156,* 158
 kinds of icons in, *137, 138, 140*
 standard color palette of, 116–117, *117,* 208
 standards of design, 36, *79,* 167–168
 as a successful 3-D interface, *29,* 102, *106*
 target monitor for, 112
Windows 95 Guide to Application Design, 209
wizards, 43, *145*
words. *See* text
writers, 14, 35–36

X

Xerox Star, 137

Y

yin and yang, 88–89, *89*